Healing From Hurt

A Memoir of Healing from Child Abuse

By Scotty O'Brien

Foreword

I have wanted to start this book many times over the past twelve years. Usually my desire peaked during a drama-filled, traumatic time, like my wedding day, the birth of my first daughter, my wife leaving me (don't worry, she came back), the birth of my second daughter, one of the many times that my parents have broken promises to one of the two aforementioned little girls, or when my mother threatened to "put a bullet through me and my old man." Oh yeah—I guess I'll pick that last one, since it's the most recent event and this time I had to get the law involved. That's always a hoot. *Yes, Your Honor, I'd like a restraining order placed against my own mother.*

What kind of family did I come from, you ask? I'd like to share my story with you. But before I start, you should know that I'm not here to write a "poor me" book—so don't feel too sorry for me. Instead, try to understand my journey. My hopes are that as some of you read these pages, you will find something in common with me, have a good laugh and/or maybe a refreshing cry, and see that there actually is light at the end of the tunnel.

I have almost forty years of abuse experience to share, and a lot of it is both painful and confusing. As I age and evaluate my life through therapy with the help of my psychologist and my family, the more I realize how screwed up my "toxic parents" really are (thank you, Dr. Susan Forward, for introducing that term in your own book *Toxic Parents*).

The one question that continuously stands out in my mind is: "Why?" Why did my dad wake me up to whip me in the second grade every night? Why did my mom beat me with the buckle end of the belt? Why did she go "on strike" and not feed me? I'd like to ask my parents: Why didn't you, or anyone else, play with me? Why did you always complain about each other/about me to me? Why couldn't I just be like the rest of the kids? Why did you always blame me? Why did you hate me so much, and, more than that, why did you have to say it? Why did you even have me? Why didn't you go ahead and have the fucking abortion that you always like to bring up? Why do you keep coming back for more? And finally, why would you threaten the life of your own child? What did I do wrong, and what did I do to deserve this? I'm supposed to be someone whom you love fully and unconditionally.

As a reader, you may feel the same way: lonely, unloved, and uncared for—like you really weren't wanted or needed. If you can relate to this emptiness, this sadness, and the feeling of being unwanted, read on. My hope is that through the stories I tell, you can find some commonalities and together, we can discover a way through it all. I don't have a therapeutic-answers section in this book; rather, I find my therapy in the writing of the stories themselves. It is my hope that you will find some of the healing that you are looking for through my life's manuscript. Please join me on my journey.

I truly believe (and know from firsthand experience) that people pass along their learned behaviors from their childhood experiences to their own children. It is the easiest road to take. Some of these behaviors are positive, and then there are all the rest. If you are picking up this book, you are most likely used to the latter: negative and hurtful feelings that you share with yourself and/or your loved ones. Not that it will make a true difference to you personally, but I am so sorry for what your parents did to you. They could have chosen another route to take than the only way they knew.

But why would parents reinvent the wheel? Why take the time to make a difference? Why waste time making the kids they made feel loved, appreciated, supported, and cared for? It didn't happen to them. Why would they spend their precious time helping someone else and stopping the unloving cycle that they learned?

Fortunately or unfortunately, the way you were raised by your parents will quite possibly be the way you bring up your children. I am not a psychologist, counselor, or therapist. I have not gone through professional training. I can share advice only from the point of view of one individual who got screwed over and shortchanged to another. I can only assume my statement about your parenting skills is on target because I was once heading down the same path that my parents traveled with me.

That was until I decided that it was time to make a difference in what I was doing. I did not want my children to miss out on the love and the caring experiences that were actually available to them and what I was truly capable of providing—as long as I was willing to make significant changes. These changes were by no means easy or quick. The road that I've traveled has been long and difficult, but I made the decision to give my children unconditional love, care, and support. It was hard to sort through all of the clouds of confusion that my toxic parents left behind, but I knew that I wanted something different for my children, though I was not sure what it was at first; I just did not want them to suffer through the same childhood experiences I had.

Paul McCartney once said, "The love you take is equal to the love you make." What a true statement! The more you get balances perfectly with the more you give. If you provide your family with love, then you can expect love in return. But if you ignore them, their wants and their needs, for too long, you should expect less or nothing in return. *You* determine what you will receive as your reward—no one else. Children are a lot smarter than you think, and they can determine who is fulfilling the needs in their family. If you are part of a family in which only one parent provides love, then you can expect your kid to lean toward the one who is meeting their needs, as children generally follow the more stable and giving of the parents who are there for them.

Now, not everyone who is reading this book has a family yet, and some may choose not to ever have one. No problem; the following stories are applicable to you as well. It is not a requirement to have children to find a need to make changes in your life. If you are single or married without children, you can still make significant changes for the benefit of the other people for whom you really care. But first and foremost, do it for the most important person: you! Those differences can help you to become great in anything: your personal life, your career, or your relationships. Everything is available for you to make it better. Go ahead and make that change!

I have learned that after you make your initial decision to become a better person, you will need to make an ongoing, conscious effort to continue down a road that you are not familiar with. This decision will be the hardest thing that you have ever done. It is so much easier to jump on the path that you already know. It is easier to talk the talk and not walk the walk. It is also easier to bullshit your way through with made-up promises to the people whom you are passing the abuse on to. But this will work for only a short while, and then you will fall back into the cycle again. I know—I have done it myself for years. It is not fair to you or to them.

Then, every once in a while, the voice inside you will cry out and ask to be heard. It may sound silly, but it is the voice of reason, asking to come out and win: *This all can't be right. Just because you learned it that way does not mean that it is all right!* So you must sort through the decisions that you are making to ensure that the ones you make are truly the right ones.

I actually wrote that last paragraph to be intentionally confusing. It is a summary of what my mind, and maybe yours, goes through every time you are trying to make the "right" decision. The only advice I can give you from my experiences is that if someone gets hurt in the process, you probably chose the wrong path. That voice of reason is there for a truly defined purpose. Listen to it closely, and you will find your way out eventually, but nothing in this process will happen quickly. You must endure the pain that you grew up with, face it, and overcome it. You cannot just bury the pain and your learned behaviors and habits and hope they will go away.

Sooner or later, the experiences that you had growing up that helped to form who you are as a person will catch up with you. There is no escaping those past experiences that you have had unless you decide to. You must make the change. Day by day, month by month, and year by year, you must stay on top and in control of your new you, in order to rebuild yourself the right way. This decision is not a sign of weakness, but a movement toward making your life, and the lives of those who share it with you, better. It will not be easy. As a matter of fact, it will be the hardest thing that you have ever faced. But in the end, when you look back and realize that you are breaking the cycle, you can be proud of yourself for what you have accomplished . . . so far.

I say "so far" for one simple reason: I believe in the idea "once abused, always abused." My mother-in-law (who is a counselor and whom I love dearly—and she didn't even make me write that) once told me that, according to a very well-known alcohol rehabilitation program, an alcoholic will always be an alcoholic. Yes, he or she may be in therapy for addiction and clean and sober for five or ten years, but that person can never drink again.

I truly believe that the same goes for the abused. You can't just undo everything that you have been taught and that has been painted into your soul; that is (fortunately or unfortunately) a part of you. An abused child will always be an abused child. It is what you do with it that will make the difference to you and your loved ones. But just remember, it will always be a continuous process, and you will probably never find a complete solution. You must never stop giving it the best you can. Even in times of anger or sadness, fight for what is right. Don't settle for less.

So let's begin our journey together. Again, remember to laugh and cry. As I write this exploration of crappy experiences, I will be doing the same. Your situations and stories may be better or worse than mine were, but we are not here to compete. We are here to share and grow.

Keep in mind that once you are ready to begin your journey, you have to make the decision to change and then stick with it. There is a long road ahead of you that will never end, so you might as well take the scenic route on the way there. Go ahead! Make yourself a better person! You will love what you can become!

Chapter 1: They Met in a Psych Ward . . . Really?

Some couples find their perfect soul mate at a coffee shop, park, bar, or library or even through another friend. That is awesome—the power of finding true love is unstoppable! But my parents had to be different. Yep, they had to one-up everybody else and beat the odds. They met in a psychological rehabilitation facility. But for the sake of this chapter's title, let's just call their meeting place a psych ward.

I cannot give you the exact details of what transpired in this fine institution, because I was not a for-sure thing yet. I have been told that my mother was in for ongoing treatments of electroshock therapy to erase a history of I don't know what. Her psychiatrist deemed this approach the perfect cure what was ailing her: instead of dealing with the problems, they just pretended they'd never happened. As you can tell, I am not too fond of this form of treatment.

My father reportedly checked in because he needed rest from an all-too-loud and obnoxious roommate who wouldn't let him get any sleep. (I'm not really sure, but whatever.) Regardless, both of my parents were hospitalized to get away from some sort of reality, to try to fix their brains, and to be sent back out into the real world to continue with their daily lives. I am not against this form of rehab, because, as you will discover in later chapters, I would end up there, too.

I don't know whether their rehab process cured them of their diagnoses, but I can tell you that my mother's bad behavior and my father's willingness to put up with it were not. I will say this many times: my mother was, and still is, psychologically ill. She was also mean. The former condition, her actual illness, was something she could not, or chose not to, control. The latter, she could—as can everyone else who has this problem. Meanness is not an excusable sickness; it's a choice.

I feel very strongly about these topics because my family has thrown around excuses for my mother's behavior for almost forty years now. My father has always said things like, "Your mother can't help her actions because of her sickness"; "Just overlook your mother's problems—she can't help it."; "She doesn't mean what she says." My response to all of this is, "Bullshit!" No one has a prescription from the doctor to be mean-spirited, mean-hearted, or mean-willed.

My mother chooses this route of destruction and anger because she would rather ignore the problem and use it as an excuse than make things better for herself and for all of her family members. Just remember this point as you read the book: my mother is always right about everything at all times.

Despite the warning signs, some way or another, my parents met and fell in love. My mother was married at the time to her second husband. This is a very interesting point because almost thirty years later, she would accuse my wife of being a "whore" and criticize her for wearing white in her own wedding. "You shacked up with Scotty for five years and wore a big ol' white poufy dress like a whore!" *Get it right, lady—it was less than a year, and her dress wasn't that poufy. And it was off-white!* I'm not sure if you can use this phrase in a published book, but LOL.

So they met, they fell in love, my mother divorced her second husband, they procreated, and here I am.

But wait, there's more! My father annually tells me the story of how, within a week of their getting married, my mother threw a pot of boiling-hot coffee at him during a fit of rage. There was a set of flying knives in there somewhere as well. A lot of mean gestures, and not a lot of loving ones, took place under that roof.

A bit further back, as my father has often told me, a little voice inside his head told him not to say "I do" at the justice of the peace's altar on their wedding day. I think a lot of men experience this moment, but this particular message was truly divine intervention; the Greek gods, Buddha, and the pope were all trying to dial in and give him a good piece of advice. But just think: if he had followed it, I wouldn't be here now to tell you my story. So maybe it truly was destiny that brought my parents together.

Over the next couple of years, they moved around from place to place after my father was laid off from his work during the early 1970s. They worked for a high-end hotel chain and lived in the furnished apartments that their employer offered them. My mother had a knack for firing people and making guests angry. She was great at her career choice!

Sometime in 1972, my parents got drunk, ate a bunch of raw oysters, and got it on, right around the time my father's warehouse called him back to work and they moved back to my hometown of St. Louis, Missouri.

My mother has told me repeatedly that during her pregnancy, my father wanted her to have an abortion. Maybe he was trying to save me from what was to come. In any case, it turned out to be a good weapon for my mother to use against my father over the next forty years. You will see as you continue to read that this is only one of many things that you should never say to your child.

I should tell you that I am both laughing out loud and crying at the same time while I type these thoughts. I cannot help what transpired to get the stork to drop me off at this desirable location, but these are things that really happened—sad, but real. I know a lot more went on during the pre-Scotty years, but I'm here to tell you *my* story, and I hope you will laugh and cry with me. Now, back to the drama at hand.

My father and mother were living in an undesirable neighborhood in a very unsafe part of town. I was born on August 21, 1973, into this warm and affectionate family, and can still remember a few key moments in my early life.

The house that we occupied was the first that my father had bought in his career. It was extremely small—only five rooms—with white siding and green shutters. It also had a little fenced-in backyard. Throughout it were hardwood floors and the constant smell of fresh cigarette smoke from both of my parents. Great thing for a kid with severe asthma, huh?

I had a Mr. Potato Head four-wheeler that I rode around inside and banged into the walls of what I called the "doory-bell house," so named because I would go outside and ring the doorbell for fun. I also know that our desirable neighbors to the left were three career women entrenched in the oldest female profession in the Bible—and had the offspring to prove it.

I also clearly remember a radio tower outside my bedroom with a bright red beacon that shone throughout the night. This was the nightlight that put me in slumber mode during the first three years of my life. I don't really remember my parents reading stories to me or playing with me a lot, but I do remember that red light. (Please also note that the red light had nothing to do with the ladies of the night next door— just a coincidence.)

Looking back on my childhood, I can understand why I insisted on having more than one child of my own: there was no way I was going to allow that kind of loneliness to exist under my roof. Having more children may or may not be the correct answer, but it did help in my particular situation. My girls may not always get along, but they do love each other. Between my wife and me, and the fact that they always keep each other busy, loneliness is not an issue in our home.

I sometimes reflect on having two children of my own and cannot comprehend how my parents did not have the desire to play with, explore, and teach or pass on their positive experiences to their child. They would rather spend their hellish marriage making their lives and the lives of everyone around them miserable. I wonder continuously why they had me in the first place. What a sad thought to ever enter a child's mind—no matter what age he or she is.

There is only so much that comes to mind from my early years that I can write about. I used to think that it would not make a difference to a baby if his or her parents got along or not, because said baby would not remember anything anyway. Dead wrong!

In fact, even early arguments that my wife and I had had a direct impact on our first baby girl. Always remember that what you do as a couple will fall on your children's hearts and souls, because they can sense what's going on. Although they are somewhat resilient at that age, they are still tiny sponges soaking up the atmosphere around them.

As you can probably tell from these initial anecdotes, my parents never have found, and almost assuredly never will find, a common, peaceful ground. This understanding has truly affected both me and my offspring. It was neither fair nor kind that I did not have a chance to determine my own mode of transport, but rather had to endure my parents' "ride of life." But, as you will see, anything can get better. It may be a long journey to get there, but you can always make it.

Eventually, my parents came to the conclusion that it was time to move from this fine locale out to the country and get a breath of fresh air. Get ready—the ride has only just begun.

Chapter 2: Abusive Parents Start with Each Other (and a Little Advice)

In the last chapter, I spoke to the fact that abusive parents (as well as the kind that I am not used to) have a strong impact on their children's lives as they pass on their gifts of anger, hatred, rage, violence, and downright meanness. I understand that these may be very strong words, but even stronger are the repercussions that come from these learned and passed-on behaviors. Your beautiful and precious offspring, whom you fawned over for the first couple of years, will sooner or later grow up to become a direct product of their environment. The atmosphere in which you rear your children will set in motion a lifetime of experiences, whether good or bad, and will help determine what kind of people they become.

It must have been sad for my mother and father to have grown up not feeling wanted, getting yelled at all the time, and being blamed for everything during their formative years. I can only assume this is what happened, based on the stories that I have heard and on their actions that I witnessed in my younger years. But somehow they made it through—and then transferred their learned behaviors to yours truly. The cycle continued on and only grew worse with time.

My parents came from entirely different backgrounds. My father has said many times that he was the black sheep of his family, southeastern Missourians who either picked cotton or sharecropped. They were poor in money and in love. When he used to take me to Grandma's and Grandpa's, before they both passed, the adults would talk about religion and politics (most of which they made up). A lot of praying happened, as my father was trying to, and eventually did, convert his parents to Christians. The kids would either play by themselves or get yelled at by Grandpa for leaving the door open and letting the cold/hot air out and trying to cool/heat the outside. It was always so lonely when I went out to visit as a kid; I could feel the cold and rigid emptiness in that house. The one night I ever slept there, I was up all night, terrified, watching a dusty grandfather-clock pendulum swing back and forth. The whole environment was a true representation of the famous painting *American Gothic*. The only good memories that I can conjure up are the clicking of my grandma's fingernails together in my ear to get me to fall asleep. Great trick! I also enjoyed seeing my cousin come in from the Philippines every couple of years; he was the brother I never had.

My father told me a couple of stories about his own lonely childhood. He stayed down in the basement of their farm home, and one night a burglar walked right past him as he was supposedly asleep—an experience that would certainly be scary for a child of any age. There was also a story of two of the brothers getting into a fight and swinging axes at each other over some topic or another. Evidently, no one got hurt. You know, typical boy stuff.

My mother's mother was quite the opposite. I could never wait to go to Grandma's house! I never met my maternal grandfather and never heard much about him, but Grandma was an amazingly sweet, loving, and caring woman who liked to give hugs and tell me how much she loved me. She could quote Bible verses and tell stories. She never once raised her hand or her voice to me—it was so different from my parents' house. No utensils were thrown and no curse words were shouted. She was the best! It was one of the very few places that I felt safe, and at home, when I was growing up.

Had it not been for this grandmother, I would also not have developed an understanding of the true beauty of God. I would have had only the distorted view that my parents instilled in me, as they preferred to use the Almighty as more of a weapon to achieve what they wanted through threats, rather than to explain the love that He truly stands for.

What happened to the rest of that family? Almost all of them have diagnosed mental disorders. There is constant drama among them, and any and all get-togethers have some jagged edge associated with the experience, so my wife and I finally chose to remove our own family completely from any interaction with them. Our lives have been much more peaceful since. Besides, I can create enough drama in my own house without adding any outside heat to the fire.

Then there's my mother, who does not fit the definition of a family mold whatsoever. She is special in an evil sort of way—angry and mean. I have always wondered where these qualities come from and how I might make them go away. But no matter how hard I try, how many times I go back for more, and how many times she comes up with an excuse, the story always has the same unhappy ending. Her family may have issues, but they are (mostly) not as mean as she is. I have asked around over the years, and no one can pinpoint where this unacceptable attitude originated.

I can recall my parents arguing repeatedly in front of me, telling me about the other's faults or just blaming me for the wrongs in their lives. I am not sure what was worse: the verbal and physical abuse I endured, or the unpredictability that came with their actions. I never knew what I would get next or how it was to be delivered; I just knew that whatever was to come would not be a trophy experience.

If you bring a child into this wonderful world, there are a couple of rules that you should follow. First, treat others as you want to be treated. Give love without expecting anything in return. We all hope that if we give love, then we can expect love in return. If you give someone a pile of crap, then you may just end up with a roll of toilet paper.

Second, avoid at all costs involving your child in your arguments with your significant other. These conversations are private and, honestly, none of the kid's business. What happens between two consenting adults should stay that way. You are a couple because you chose to be together. It is inappropriate and destructive to place the child in the middle of your problems. Just because that innocent child, adolescent, or adult is available for you to take an easy shot at, do not do it! Remove the little person from the situation, accept responsibility for your circumstances, and deal with them accordingly. Don't pass the buck!

Always be gentle with your child, not just physically but also emotionally. Children are very delicate individuals who require tender loving care (thank you, Elvis!) and support through their hopefully long and fruitful lives. Remember, you are not the only thing that they have to deal with. Growing up, school, emotions, hormones, and especially their snot-nosed, backstabbing little friends are all very real, very difficult problems that they will face. You made them—now it's your job to be there for them, and to help them succeed.

Along the same lines falls my opinion on the notion of tough love. The misconception of teaching your child a lesson through another hard-won lesson is ridiculous. Of course kids have to learn on their own, but make sure that you give them the tools and advice they may request or may not even know they need to survive life. You might not believe their anthill problems are as serious and overwhelming as yours are, but to them, the same set of issues may feel like Mount Everest. So try to put yourself in their shoes.

Finally, never get physical with your children; doing will teach them nothing but the idea that violence and anger are a valid way to deal with a negative situation. Some of you may think that I am being too soft and gentle on this matter, but if you correct the situation with love and show that you truly and genuinely care, you will gain the respect and friendship of that child, versus the fear and mistrust that come from raising your hand because you are angry. Remember, you're the one who's fired up—don't take your anger out on the little one whom you love so much.

There is also a misconception that having a child will solve marital issues and somehow make life easier. I am here to tell you from personal experience that that is not the case. Children are nothing less than a blessing, but they are constant work. If you have children already and are breaking some of the aforementioned rules, swallow your pride and find a way to help yourself become a better parent and person first. If you don't have children and are daring to think that those little gifts will cure what ails you and your relationship, think again.

My parents did not follow any of these rules. They made up their own as they went along. Unqualified, inappropriate, angry, and abusive behaviors were the norm in my family. And my parents' abuse wasn't restrained to their only child; they abused each other constantly as well, with threats, violence, insults, and hatred. Literally each day and night was filled with constant confrontations, fighting, yelling, insults, and, later in life (when I was seven or eight years old), physically moving from one house and community to another. Amid all of this mental, emotional, and physical turmoil, I had a difficult time calling any of our houses a home. None of them was safe, and I had no place to hide.

Besides the hot coffee and the knife throwing, there was not a lot of physical violence going on between my parents. The main abuse that my parents subjected each other and me to was verbal and emotional. Nothing could ever be said in a gentle and loving way. There always had to be some abrasion, insult, or blame added to the mix. Almost everything that came out of their mouths was intended to inflict some type of penetrating wound, and it really hurt everyone.

As I have aged and spoken with friends and family about my experiences over the years, I have come to the conclusion that I would much rather have been physically abused than to have been subjected to the mental, emotional, and verbal abuse of which I was a victim. Bruises on the outside will go away after a week or two, but the cancerous, deep-penetrating wounds caused by verbal abuse take years to heal, if they ever do. One of my best friends always says, "Keep your words soft and sweet, because someday you might have to eat them." True that, Cali.

So I will wrap up this chapter with a piece of advice to all you couples out there, with children or not: your relationship needs to be in good order for you to have an even better relationship with your children. In my worst impression of Yoda, "Be mindful of things you say, you should." In other words, watch what you say not only to yourself, but to each other. Words can be very damaging to the soul of the one whom you claim to love dearly. And you have to start with each other before you can be good role models for your little one.

You have heard people say that if you cannot say something nice, then don't say anything at all. This does not mean that you cannot have a disagreement and a discussion about the topic, but there is no reason to get mean or violent with your partner. Humans are bound to have different beliefs and views, and that's healthy. Verbally and physically beating up your mate just because you don't agree with him or her is not right.

If you are so small that you have to physically abuse the person you are with, man or woman, then go take a break for a while and figure out what the hell is wrong with you before you put another bruise on that person. And stop using the excuse that my parents used to beat the hell out of me: "I can't help it." Bullshit! If you are this person, then go pick a fight with someone three or four times your size, and don't fight back.

What I am trying to say is that there is no need—or excuse—for physical violence. If the rage within you is that strong, then leave before your fire gets burning. Make a solemn promise to yourself that you will never again touch your partner—or anyone else—in a violent way, and then stick with it. If you can't be man/woman enough to keep your hands to yourself, then get the fuck out. And don't even think about touching your children!

I'm going now to have a cigarette, and I don't even smoke.

Chapter 3: My Swing Set and the Clouds

Long, warm, breezy, sunny afternoons, while birds flew around and overhead. And not just any birds—those trusting little brown ones that will come close to you if you have bread crumbs to share. Fifteen acres of weeded field that I got to ride the sun-washed and dulled red farm tractor on, with a brush hog pulling behind. That stupid barking dog across the street. Plenty of big, fluffy clouds that all formed familiar shapes. Gasp in, breathe out.

Those are some of the first childhood memories that I can really get my mind around—the good ones. What I also remember is that I was very lonely and did not have many people to play with, either kids or adults. My life and soul were empty; there was nothing for me to give, because I was never given to.

My father worked the night shift at a warehouse in St. Louis, so I was stuck at home with my mother for the start of my growing-up years. We had just moved out to the "sticks," as my mother called it, on a long and dusty gravel road. We lived in a basement house with very few windows for outside light. A tar roof, concrete, and dark-wood paneling comprised the decor that welcomed what few guests would visit us. Until my father finished the upstairs portion of the house, it always reminded me of the house that he grew up in: lonely.

My mother hardly ever played with me; instead she sat at the kitchen table with a pack of Virginia Slims cancer sticks. She almost never needed a lighter, as she chain-smoked away her days. I know now why I liked being outside on that swing set so much: fresh air! *You* try living underground in a nuclear bunker for a while and see how stale the air you breathe becomes.

Next to the kitchen, my father had a tool shop, where our tall upright freezer was also housed. I loved to play on my dad's workbench and create (i.e., destroy) things with leftover scraps of two-by-fours and nails. I was also a master at fixing unbroken toys. The minute I got a remote-control car for my birthday, I took it apart and lubricated the gears just to make sure it would run smoothly. Boys!

I also built a lot of wooden crosses for the pulpit in my room, as I was destined to be a preacher like Jim Bakker or Jimmy Swaggart. My sermons always involved Bible verses and ended with "The truth is the truth, and that's the truth." No one ever attended my church.

I do remember one time when my mother played with me. I had set up a fine-dining restaurant in my room and served my mother a well-prepared paper-plate meal. This experience was soon interrupted by her and my father getting into it over something I can't recall, and that was the end of that play session.

Our living room had a horizontal cabinet stereo with a radio, a turntable, and an eight-track. My early favorites were the Eagles' "Take It to the Limit," Joe South's "Games People Play," and a song called "They're Coming to Take Me Away" by Napoleon XIV, released in 1966. This song was about some fella who was on his way to the funny farm, where life was beautiful all the time. Look it up on YouTube, and you'll understand why I'm smiling as I write this. I think my dad played the song as a staple just to get to my mother.

Outside, we had a garden where my dad grew strawberries, corn, and tomatoes. I actually enjoyed working with him (as much a kid would), because it meant that I got to spend time with my father, or anyone. The more I think about it, the more I can understand why I tolerated my parents' verbal and emotional abuse: I felt like a weird outcast, and I was just looking for anyone to play with me. Humans are not made to be held at arm's length, with no one to love and nurture us.

The last thing that stands out in my mind about that property was my dog's house and the dog himself, Spirit, who made it away safely from the neighbors at the previous house before they could have him for dinner. I would climb into his getaway, hug him, and talk to him for hours at a time. Dogs truly are a boy's best friend.

I filled my days with swinging back and forth on a small and rusty play set that faced the woods, talking to Spirit, and finding shapes in the clouds. Our horizon was filled with trees and a lot of blue. Not a big, Montana type of sky, but an open one to fill with hopes and dreams. I really did not understand all of the yelling inside the house at the time, but I can remember the sky vividly. It was very quiet outside.

My wife, who has been with me through thick and thin and has a great ability to evaluate my thoughts and my feelings, has always said that my parents and I talk *at* each other, not *to* each other. I now understand what she means. When I was growing up, there was no filter, softness, or care in my parents' words, most of which were just verbal vomit; there was always anger and downright meanness. Their verbal and nonverbal cues always included something negative, deceptive, or unfulfilling.

Christmas was always my favorite holiday. I knew nothing would ever change in my house, but I could still enjoy other people's families who were filled with the spirit of the holidays. I loved that Maxwell House commercial! I got to help my dad set up our tree while my mom accused him of a continuous and fabricated list of atrocities. We played the same Christmas record over and over every year. In fact, from the day we erected the tree until the day we took it down, I would lie on the sofa and watch the lights flash off and on in the threesome of red plastic bells that we hung up on the wall every year.

We never made cookies or did puzzles or anything truly memorable as a family. If any kind of game was ever played out, it was between my father and me. To his credit, he did teach me Battleship, checkers, and Chinese checkers, but these activities were, of course, accompanied by my mother's complaining about something not getting done while he spent time with his son.

To this day, I spend the month before Christmas in pure emotional bliss, trying to squeeze every ounce of happiness that I can muster from everyone around me. Now that I think back to that point in my life, I guess I had started to develop a protective shell of some kind so I wouldn't end up a total waste. You may think that a four-year-old can't feel and figure things out about his or her surroundings, but I am living proof that that notion is wrong.

I remember getting to open presents and then playing with them alone for as long as my young interest would hold. At least my parents would watch me open them. It was one of the few occasions they always seemed excited to share with me. Still, I could feel the atmosphere in the room getting ready to erupt at any time. My poor dad! My wife wonders why I love this holiday so much; in hindsight, it was the only time of year when anyone paid any real attention to me.

The best part of the Christmas season could never come soon enough: my sister's house! We would all load up into the family's green Buick and head toward the city in the smoke-filled car—a gasp-inducing experience. But after what seemed like days in that toxic space, we would finally arrive at our destination, and we'd be all smiles for the rest of that day.

My sister and her husband were amazing. They were a fun and loving bunch, a real family. I'm not sure if my sister ever knew this, but my parents and I would actually argue on the way home about why we couldn't be a family like theirs. They had two boys who were a blast to spend time with. The older typically played with the younger one, and they were both nice to me. There was no judging or finger pointing at that house, no anger—just love.

My sister's husband also came from an extremely loving family. The word that comes to mind to summarize his parents is "fair." In addition, no matter what happened, they always seemed to be nice people, warm and welcoming, even to my parents.

My sister is actually my half sister—a product of my mom and her earlier husband. I don't know much about what her childhood was like, but I imagine that she must have had empty moments, like I did. After all, the apple doesn't fall far from the tree. She, like anyone else, has her own set of difficulties to deal with, but she and her husband make a great team, and somehow they've figured out how to make one hell of a great family.

I always wished that I had another sibling to share my childhood with who was closer to my own age. My sister and I were twenty years apart and did not have anything in common until later in life. I have always wondered whether my parents would have been the same, or worse, with another child. Would they have loved the other sibling more or less than they loved me? All I can promise is that there would have been an unfair favorite. Oh well—I had to just figure it out alone. (Hey, I deserve at least one "poor me" moment in all this shit.)

My sister's boys and I, and our cousin who lived down the street, would play Atari or form our own Kiss rock band or run around the neighborhood or play Monopoly. Everything was safe at my sister's home. Sometimes the other boys would all go outside and play sports and I would watch. My father never played ball or any sport with me, so I was never good at physical activities. I could go on and on about my excursions with this amazing household. Simply stated, they were amazing! The best! I could not wait to get there, and was extremely sad when I had to leave.

These were also the times when my mother's family would get together at my sister's house for the holidays. They all seemed to be fine back then, but as the years progressed, the truth of their stunted emotional mentality became apparent. Except for one of my aunts, those brothers and sisters all have issues—*serious* issues. Whatever it was that caused these problems, it wasn't good.

After we all exchanged gifts and headed back home in the green smoke machine, I always retreated to my lonely room and thought—a lot. *Why won't anyone play with me? Why do they always yell at each other and at me? Why did they even have me?* These are pretty deep topics for a five-year-old to face, but they are what raced through my mind—and I promise you that your own kids are a lot smarter and more perceptive than you will ever imagine.

It is sad and embarrassing for me to think about anyone else's having to go through what I did. Between the emotional emptiness and the verbal and physical abuse that characterized my household, I was never quite sure which direction I should head. It was always a lose-lose game. All I wanted was to be happy like the rest of the kids I saw. They didn't have this baggage to tolerate; why did I? Why did I have no one? Why did I have nowhere to go or run to? Why did I have no one to rely on? Why did I have no shoulder to cry on?

I urge you to think deeply now about the effects that your actions could have on your offspring, and about how they will remember their young lives once they have grown up. Mine sucked. Yours probably did, too. Let's make it better for us and for them.

Chapter 4: "Thirty Years—I'm Going on Strike!"

This chapter will be about even more painful memories that I can conjure, and that took place at the very same address where the previous chapter's incidents occurred. I was five, time was passing (slowly), and my parents were gradually moving from bad to worse, in terms of both their relationship and their anger and hatred toward me. I do remember thinking about my parents a lot around that age and trying to figure out why Mommy and Daddy shouted at each other so much. I also recall wondering, *Why am I getting yelled at, too? I didn't do anything wrong.* The whole story line is really screwed up.

I was going into kindergarten, but instead of spending my precious time worrying about which tree to climb and where, exactly, I had put my toy truck or when I would get to play with my best friend, I was analyzing. I was trying to figure out something that was not even mine. I was worrying about my parents' problems and wondering if this was the way other mommies and daddies got along. I also remember wondering if they would stay together or not—a very scary thought for a small child to contemplate, as marriage is supposed to be the strongest bond that a kid can rely on. This makes me very angry as I reflect, because I had already lost one of the gifts a child growing up is supposed to receive: childhood itself. I had to mostly raise myself to become what little I am today.

My parents stole from me one of the most valuable rites of passage. Instead of playing with and breaking things, I was trying to figure out all of the "whys" of my family's dynamic. I could not associate or share my inner feelings with friends, because I did not know how to make those bonds last. Yes, I could always go up and talk to someone my age and hit it off, but those associations lasted only a short while. Living out in the sticks made things even harder, because the very few kids who lived near me would all too soon alienate the "weird" kid. I played alone—a lot.

If, as parents, you can relate to any of the above, then please work on your problems and keep your beautiful babies away from them. It was not fair for me and is not fair for my children to deal with the punishing anguish that I went through. Let your kids grow up in a carefree and joyous environment, not one in which they're trying to figure out what the hell is wrong with their parents. They did not do anything wrong, so you cannot blame them just because you and your partner are trying to figure out your lives. Go see a counselor or get some help—just leave them out of it. And if you think for a moment that kids don't "get it" at their young age, think again! Please let them enjoy their youthful innocence while they can, before they have to deal with the problems of their world.

From the start of my life as a student, I was very good friends with my principal. I had the privilege of visiting him on a regular basis, usually in the late-morning hours of the school day. He always welcomed me warmly into his office and invited me to remain standing, before he asked me to drop my pants (which I thought was weird even back then, too) and receive his "blessing" via a wooden paddle across my backside. I think the lashes went on until I started to cry, and then I got a few more for good measure. Corporal punishment is what they called it back then— now it's referred to as child abuse.

As you might guess, my parents only added fuel to the fire. When I came home from school after a day of embarrassment and humiliation, I had to endure round two of retribution so that I could pay the piper at home as well. My parents' favored method of whipping/beating the hell out of me was with a flyswatter or a leather belt—whichever was closer at hand. I guess they and the principal became good friends over the first years of my schooling—they had a lot in common.

As I've stated, I did not have many friends in my school years. The couple of friends my age I did have at school, now that I look back on it, were all facing their own problems at home or somewhere; something was wrong. Kids associate with people whom they can find things in common with, and sometimes they find someone, usually older than they are, who they feel can resolve their problems somehow. My older daughter has a knack for doing the same: she can sniff out people who are like her, who have been through what she has in one way or another. Poor thing.

I did pretty well academically. I was an honors student in elementary school, as I was "gently coerced by my parents, especially my father," to do well. However, I don't think the educational value of my performance was the important piece to my family, so much as the control they had over my studies and me was. It seemed as though they wanted to control every aspect of my life but did not really care about the outcome or result of it either way. This pattern is another telltale sign of abusive parents.

I am not sure of the specifics of the arrangement that they set up, but somehow my education became my father's deal. He would come and review my grades for the day and would decide what to do next. I cannot recall if the breaking point for him was a B or C grade, but if I received anything lower, it was punishment time.

My father would wake me up when he got home from work at 3:00 AM and spank me until he was happy with my response. He would then send me back to bed in tears, without any consolation. I now assume he believed this routine would teach me to get better grades and keep me in the honors program. As I was only six or seven years old then, I didn't get his memo. I don't have a lot more to say about this matter, but I did learn that it is not the way I want to teach my children the importance of an education.

I can specifically remember my mom's getting involved with my educational process one time as well. She was not as consistent as my father was, but she did make her point . . . well. (Trust me.) However, she finally stepped in to protect me—one of the very few times she did—and my nightly beatings subsided after a few months. My father eventually lost interest in my grades and decided to move on to something else—probably her.

When I began slacking a bit on my schoolwork, I decided it was best that I protect my parents—and my ass—from the unpleasant news. I remember that my parents were on one of their month-long battles with each other, and I won the prize! I had hidden my schoolwork, and my disappointing grades, in the culvert at the end of our long gravel driveway. I'm guessing that went on for a month or so, because the papers that I had placed in the culvert stopped the flow of water from going through.

We must have been having a particularly rainy season, because my dad found it necessary to fix the culvert on a Saturday. I know this because he was home all day. He did his husband duties and restored the flow. When my parents discovered the papers, all hell broke loose and my mother beat the living shit out of me. It was the first, and really the only, time I can remember her punishing me physically—but it was an episode that I will never forget.

She asked me about the papers, and I told her that I was keeping them for some other kid on the school bus, who happened to be named Scotty O'Brien, too, and who, even more oddly, had the same handwriting as mine. My mother took me into the guest bedroom, locked the door, and began whipping me with the whole leather belt, buckle and all. I'm not sure how long the session lasted, but I do remember bleeding on the carpet in the bedroom and getting yelled at for that as well.

The lesson that I learned from all this? I'm not sure if I actually did learn anything; I just remember wondering how and why my own mother could do something like that to me. I also recall my feelings of rage and resentment growing stronger, both toward my parents, for what they did to me, and, doubly, toward whoever was not doing anything to protect me.

You would think that a child this age would be too young to analyze and contemplate such things, but trust me: based on my own experience and on my close monitoring of my older daughter, these young ones can figure it out. They know what's going on. So I recommend that you do your best to make their memories positive and happy. Oh yeah—I never went near that culvert again, so I guess I did learn a lesson.

As life went on, so did the abuse. My mother, who had held some rewarding career positions— beautician, onion-ring-factory worker, hotel manager—came to the conclusion that she was going to retire when I was seven or eight.

My mother decided that she had had enough of cooking, cleaning, and the general upkeep in our home, so she went "on strike" after thirty years of hard life, as she called it. The thirty-year time frame never made any sense to me, because she was older than that, but the concept was even worse. She essentially decided that she was not going to lift a finger around the house again—she had had enough! True to her word, she completely stopped being a wife, parent, domestic helpmate, and caregiver and focused her attentions on bitching about everything. She was great at that.

My dad switched his shifts at the warehouse from night to morning so I could eat and be taken care of. That was the good part, because I got to spend more time with my father, and our bond improved. The closest we got to gourmet meals for the next two or three years may have been potpies and TV dinners, but it was something. Meanwhile, my mother just sat at the kitchen table, smoking one cigarette right after the other, ignoring herself and her family as life went by. Her "retirement" never did end—she made a point and stuck with it. The moment she officially rejected all work, it became everyone else's problem.

The final story that I will share from this stage of my life can be embarrassing to a child and to his parents as well, and one that I do not recall clearly. I was called into the counselor's office at school and questioned for who knows what. All I remember well is the question that started a whole mess for my parents: "Scotty, does your mom or dad beat you?"

"Yes, they beat the hell out of me all of the time."

At least, that's what they told me.

To make a very long story short, we were visited by Child Protective Services, but my parents covered up the incident very well and things just got worse after that for me. I truly don't know too much information about this piece of my life, as it was either hidden well from me or simply glossed over very quickly. That's probably better in the end, anyway—I still have plenty more to go.

There was no escaping what I was going through, no way out of what was happening in my life—it just was what it was. Kids don't know that they can escape from or get help in a situation like this; they feel as if they are just stuck. The same is true of the abusive relationship of a couple: one spouse either is too frightened by or does know any other way to be than the situation that he or she is in, and thus is bound by the chains of whatever abuse is holding him or her there.

My wife and I have had a hard and long road to travel, and we are still on a two-lane, country dirt path. But, and this is the most important part, we have made progress. We have gotten better. I have been blessed to find a mate who will support me (although it is a hard pill to swallow) on my journey to make something great out of nothing at all. Thank you so much for that, Wife!

My older daughter has witnessed and still does witness my struggles left over from my childhood. I only recently decided to make myself better for my family and me. Thankfully, they have supported me and put up with all of my bullshit during this process. I hold them in the highest regard for doing this and cannot thank them enough. In return, it is my job to do the best I can for them. You can do the same—give it all you've got. The rewards are amazing!

This is all good news for my readers, because you are getting a real-time story, a work that is still in progress. I will invite you again to please use my misfortunes to your advantage to make your life better than you could ever imagine.

Chapter 5: A Little Bit More About My Parents and Their Families, and Jesus, Too!

Physical, emotional, and verbal abuse are handed down from generation to generation just like other aggressive and destructive diseases, such as cancer. The disease of abuse can have traumatic physical and/or emotional effects. No matter what age the victim is, it destroys our soul when someone whom we love and trust dishonors us, but the effects are even worse for a child, who has no understanding of how or why the abuse is happening and wonders simply, *How could my mommy or daddy do this to me?* It is up to the abused to make the definitive decision to stop the cycle and the disease from spreading to the next generation.

As I stated in this book's foreword, my parents were raised in two completely different environments that nonetheless somehow complemented each other. My father came from a lonely and empty house where love was not shared freely and there was no true camaraderie among the siblings or the parents.

My father once told me that "the reason people had children in the old days was to have more hands to work in the fields." In reflection, I can see that this attitude and the atmosphere it engendered was rampant throughout my father's family. His parents were extremely hard workers who did not receive many rewards for their years of continuous labor; working in the fields for someone else was merely a means of putting food on the table, and not much else. Based on the stories that have been passed on to me, I think they coexisted to make ends meet. Education or furthering themselves was not a priority with most of the family; they simply did what they had to do to survive.

Now, all of that being said, this family is not without its charms, though you have to dig deep to find them. They do have family reunions and get-togethers all the time to stay in touch with each other, but at these functions, there is a lack of warmth and expression of feelings among most of the participants. There are also a few apparent signs of abuse, including some neglect and bullying, in my father's immediate family.

As I stated earlier, the personality of the family is similar to the atmosphere in the painting *American Gothic*, in which somewhere behind the subjects' cold, rigid, and emotionless faces is a sense of care. As this is an aging bunch, the lines of the brothers' and sisters' poor and lonely lives are now etched into their faces and souls.

My dad has told me many times that he was the "black sheep" of the family, and his role as such is palpable at these family get-togethers. There are stories of his parents locking him in their basement for short stints. He has also told me that his father (remember, it all rolls downhill) made him feel undesired and unwanted—essentially, that he was nothing more than a burden. He left home at an early age to find work and, I suspect, to escape what was missing in his life.

My father seems to try really hard to fit in socially, but he just doesn't have the communication skills necessary to talk to people one-on-one. He often sugarcoats his conversations with dangerous humor involving paranoia, racial slurs, bad politics, and the less fortunate in the United States. This paranoia seems to dictate his entire life.

My father travels alone on vacations out West a couple of times a year, for weeks at a time. I enjoy going with him on some of these trips, but my schedule keeps me from joining him often. He tells me that he is content with being alone, but I don't buy it. He and I are very alike in the fact that we need some sort of contact and conversations with other beings. As I get older, I have chosen to participate in healthy relationships over whatever creeps in and out of the journey of life. His choice of acquaintances and friends outside of his family usually comprise a less desirable audience.

I have said throughout this book that abuse is passed on from parents to their children, generation to generation, in a continuous and learned cycle. As I examine my father's history closely, I believe he was a victim of bullying by his siblings and peers and ignored by his parents. In short, he was just not wanted. If a child is given nothing from his parents or loved ones, then he/ she has nothing to return. He was different, and this difference was not to be accepted. So I believe that he had to fill this emptiness with something—and that something was anger and hatred for others.

I also believe that my father has picked up additional abusive and mean habits from my mother. My father may not have come from a background of love and affection, but I also believe he and his family lacked the hate or meanness my mother had brewing inside her. With her, the geyser was always ready to erupt, and that caught on with my father as well.

My maternal grandfather was a typical hardworking American trying to make ends meet. Evidently, he enjoyed keeping his wife warm at night, as they had many offspring to prove it. They also, unfortunately, lost an unusual amount of kids in the birthing process. He passed away before I was born, while he was working on heavy machinery. Don't worry, my days are numbered because of the crappy health problems that have been passed on to me from both sides of my family. I don't know very much about this man, but people say he was kind and gentle.

My maternal grandmother, as I have already stated, was nothing less than a perfect angel. She was very religious (serving as a role model for me in that sense), loving, temper-free, concerned, humble, and just about any other adjective you can think of that says you would like her to be your grandmother, too.

So, if these two were such perfect parents, what the hell happened to their kids? I cannot pinpoint why their children turned out the way they are, but there were a lot of psychological problems running throughout this bloodline. My mother is not the only one who required psychological care, but she was the worst of the bunch. Nervous tics, bouts of anger, vindictive streaks, and even some downright hatred would sum up a good part of the relationships between her and most of her brothers and sisters, who, in their later years, have battled over such topics as finances, interfamily theft, and their children. Vindictive, angry, spiteful, jealous, using, and mean are words that describe my mother's side of the family. Although they were not always like this, over the years, something has brought out the worst in this particular bunch of individuals. It could be the onset of an older age or just the dynamics of this family tree, but it is hard to imagine it getting any worse.

For the most part, the spouses of these siblings deserve sainthood in the ever after. You cannot even begin to imagine the punishment that they have gone through in one form or another over the years. There is no way that these folks knew what they were signing up for when they said, "I do!" So, where did the aforementioned descriptions come from? Let's dive in and explore together.

My mother has deep-rooted psychological problems that have kept her both depressed and angry her whole life. She has been diagnosed with schizophrenia, borderline personality disorder, psychosis, and severe manic depression, which is the same damn thing as bipolar disorder. Yep, I got lucky and won the genetic lottery on this one, folks!

There are not really signs of physical abuse in this family, just a lot of verbal and emotional abuse.

There have also been some stories of sexual abuse between various family members that have seemed to make their mark on the victims as they have gotten older.

One particular story that I would like to share provides an example of the inappropriateness of some of the members of my mother's extended family. My wife and first daughter went to visit my mother and meet one of my uncles, whom I had not seen in at least thirty years. Upon entering the house, my wife said hello, and, without blinking an eye, the uncle said, "Does that kid still suck a titty?"

Really? How do you respond to that one? My mother laughed, and my wife and daughter left immediately, horrified and disgusted. End of story; enough said.

Thankfully, my wife, daughters, and I have been excluded for many years from any family activities because of my relationship to my mother and father, and also probably due to the fact that I refuse to engage with these individuals, as I do not want their drama to be passed along to my children. I usually don't find out about a death or sickness in the family for many months. My girls have not seen most of the family in years, and we will likely keep it that way. We have plenty of close friends who act more like family than my own and provide my children with the love and support that should come from this intricate system.

My mother and father also rant and rave about religion and continuously use it as a tool of poor lesson teaching and revenge. The Ten Commandments and other teachings of the Bible were pounded into me during my upbringing, and I thank them for that. I feel that it is a parent's obligation to provide their children with some sort of belief system to follow. It is between you and your significant other to determine which religious faith you intend to teach and pass on. Instilling religion and faith in your kids will provide them with the tools that they need for future endeavors when they have to choose between right and wrong.

Regretfully, my parents have always taken religion, as well as just about everything else in life, a step further. They use God, Jesus, and the Bible hypocritically as a set of weapons for threats and revenge. "If you don't honor and appreciate your mother and me, you'll go to hell!" "Jesus hates liars; they will have their part in the lake of fire, and you and your father will burn in it forever!"

I could go on and on with examples, but I believe my point is clear. In one breath, I would hear how much they hated this or that and then how much Jesus Christ had helped them solve this or the other problem. The God I serve is fair, loving, just, and forgiving—not to be used to my advantage to win whatever it is I am trying to accomplish—whereas my parents used religion as a "weapon of mass destruction" to put anything they did not agree with in its place.

So where do I stand on all of these words of wisdom? I am a God-fearing, Spirit-filled, Jesus-following Christian who believes fundamentally what the Bible says. That is my own choice that I have decided to make, the path I have decided to follow. I have also encouraged and tried to lead my family down the same path, but in a kinder and gentler way. I feel that your God is the most important thing in your life, with family running immediately behind. I will *not* use and abuse this amazing love as a tool to threaten my children into loving and respecting me, as my parents tried to do with me. I will provide them with a good, loving, and solid foundation and will answer questions that they may have about the higher power, but I will use religion for that which it is intended: love, kindness, and fairness.

Despite my parents' use of religious threats against me—"If you don't honor and respect your mother and me, you are going to hell!"—I agree with the Bible that you must honor your parents, and, believe it or not, I still honor mine to this day. I thank them for providing a roof over my head, a college education, and all of the basic essentials that I needed to survive. But I have a really hard time respecting them after all of the abuse that they have given as their gift to their "one and only" child.

I also think the "honor" part is for people who have *earned* a right to be honored, and if they have destroyed that predestined gift, it's not my fault. I didn't ask my parents to beat, punish, mistreat, abuse, and hate me, but they did. So where is the honor in that? Honor is defined as "honesty, fairness, or integrity in one's beliefs and actions." (Thanks, Google.)

Honor and respect have to be earned, but my parents destroyed their opportunity to reap the benefits of these gifts, by abusing them for their personal benefit and by using religion as a weapon to try to get their way. I have found the good in the religion that I have been raised on and have pushed the other, abusive pieces to the side. I think that when I go to the pearly gates, I may "prayerfully" have a pass on this one.

All this goes to prove my thinking that abuse is passed on from generation to generation. It started with my father's siblings and parents on his side, and who knows where on my mother's side. I just know, without a doubt, that they have unfairly passed the abuse on to me. I also know that I am stopping the cycle in my own family now!

I will elaborate in later chapters about my wrongdoings before I made my all-important decision.

My family has done nothing to deserve this form of hatred. I love them too much to let it go on. You should do the same: stop the cycle—now!

Chapter 6: My Dog and Me on a Moped

Now that you know a little more about my parents' background, you may have gathered that they really never got along. Some couples go through periods of disagreement (I know my wife and I do) and come to hurdles in communication that they just can't jump, climb, or even knock over. It is human nature to be an individual person with individual thoughts, feelings, and viewpoints, and sometimes this causes contention between the two parties. In these situations, a couple can agree to disagree and move on, or debate about the issue until they reach a resolution, or fight, fight, fight.

My parents always chose the third option but enhanced the choice with unhealthy hate, rage, and other emotions that were not the norm in any society. I never once witnessed a healthy discussion between my parents on any given subject that did not turn into something more. No matter what the topic, there was going to be some sort of hate-filled problem between them. Sometimes the emotions became physically violent—usually involving my mother throwing or breaking some object that meant something to someone else in the house. She rarely broke her own shit.

My father was wise enough not to get physical with her, because she always had a standing threat of calling the authorities to step in. She knew how to use her mentally disturbed card very well.

As time slowly passed, my parents continued to argue about the alignment of the sun and the moon, or whatever. They also continued their downward spiral of abuse with me. Unlike a fine wine, soup, or my sister's lasagna, things only got worse with time. Life sucked!

Finally, though I'm not sure how they made the arrangement, my mother and father decided that it was time for a much-needed break, so they separated. Thus began my parents' *constant* moving around—separate from each other, move back in with each other, and drag the kid wherever you decide to go.

This became my opportune time to start over as well, again and again, and start short relationships all over the great state of Missouri. As a child, you do not have much of a say in where you will go or with whom you will live with if your parents call it a day; you're just assigned to the one who wants to deal with you at the time and then maybe tossed around like a hot potato between the two. In my case, I had the pleasure of going with the less stable of the two and having complete chaos added to my plate of life. You guessed right—my mother.

The three of us were living in a now-finished house out in the "sticks," and we had a daily routine. As I got older, I learned to stay away from my parents as much as possible, and they reciprocated. I played alone, a lot—no one wanted to hang out with the ADHD kid who had zero social skills. Oh well—I drummed up my own form of entertainment, usually by building forts to go hide in away from the undesirables inside the smoke-filled house.

I can't pinpoint the day that we headed down to the town where my mother was born, but we did. My mother bought a single-wide brown trailer there, and we moved in to the finest trailer park that money could rent. I wasn't too sad to leave our old house, as most kids are, because I really didn't have any friends to say good-bye to. The community we moved to, in Salem, Missouri, was a nice place, where my grandmother and my aunt and uncle also resided, and things started to look up for me. It was a fresh start: since nobody knew me or what I had been through, I could begin again.

I attended the school in town and was in fifth grade at the time. We had moved in the middle of the first semester, so I had to figure out my studies and play a little catch-up, but I was actually kind of excited about the whole deal. I made a couple of acquaintances in the (trailer) park and felt like the king of the castle. The TV shows *The A-Team* and *Knight Rider* were hot back then, so we would act out the various stunt scenes, minus explosions (mostly). Michael Knight (David Hasselhoff) was (and still is) a frickin' stud!

The best part of living in Salem was that I got to spend time with my maternal grandmother. We spent many nights at her home, studying the Bible, playing games (like Mr. Mouth), and having cornbread and milk for dinner. My newfound lifestyle was so amazing, so different from what I was used to, and I loved my grandma so much, I didn't even know what to do with myself.

I have since learned that my grandmother also raised my sister for a good part of her life and did a great job doing so. My sister turned out pretty well, considering that her own mother didn't want her; our mother thought it was more important to live the party life in St. Louis than to take care of her precious firstborn. Sis, I am truly sorry for what you had to go through in life. Thank you for trying to stop the cycle of abuse that was passed on to you, and for raising your family the way people should.

My grandmother was there for me during a much-needed healing process from the wounds that my parents had already inflicted at my early age. She provided love, support and acted as a cornerstone that helped me through this tough time in my life. Unfortunately, the battle had just begun, and things were going to get much worse for yours truly.

I am not sure how often my parents would visit each other during this yearlong stint, but I do remember it being somewhat peaceful, since they were not together to argue with each other. I also remember clearly that this was the period when my mother's opinion of my father worsened and she began to share it with me liberally at the trailer. Blame, blame, and more of the same were all she could talk about. She was not as paranoid as she would become later in life—fearing that my father and I would climb a blue spruce tree to spray Mace at her through the skylight, for example—but she already had her weapons against him out and ready to whirl.

Although Salem was a wonderful place overall—pretty calm and peaceful, dead center in the middle of the Missouri Bible Belt, full of friendly, good people—I had the same underlying problems there that I have had my whole life. The problems, of course, were my lack of skills in keeping the friends that I made. Again, the "weird" kid had to suffer. And it only got worse the older I became.

Eventually, my parents decided to somehow patch up their differences and pack up our belongings and move to yet another part of the state. Although their decision was understandable, because my dad worked in St. Louis and his drive to his job from Salem would have been three hours each way, this also marked the end of the *only* stable time in my young life that I can conjure. It was all downhill from there, as things were about to go from bad to worse. I did not have any input whatsoever in our living arrangements—we just packed up our shit and moved . . . to another trailer park. I was in the middle of sixth grade by then, and they uprooted me away from the few friendships I had worked so hard to develop.

O'Fallon, Missouri, was known as the most evil town in the great state at the time; there was always a weird feel to this community. And things at home were still heading south. My parents continued to argue and hate on each other and never had the courtesy to hide it from their child. I never invited anyone over to our trailer, as my parents would surely have embarrassed me with their meanness toward each other and toward me.

Still, some good things did come of this fine living establishment: I discovered rap music and got to play doctor with the female neighbor across the street. Ah, memories! (I won't go into the last activity on that list, but I can remember it pretty well: Prince was playing, and we were nervous as hell. That's enough of that story.) Most important, I met Mike, my best friend in the whole wide world. I played at his trailer, we had sleepovers, and we grew up together through our developmental years. I got really close with Mike's whole family, too. His mom became my mom, and she and Mike's dad were there for me as they were for their own son.

I spent a lot of time playing with his other friends, too, and even though they picked on me at times, Mike usually stood up for me. He was one of a kind. I don't ever remember really sharing my home life with him, probably because I was too young to confide in someone, but he made the nightmare of my home life go away every day amid all of our new adventures together. He was just fun! We traded stuff constantly, and he was always making bets with me (although he must have known I couldn't win most of them, since I usually got shafted in the process).

Finally, I had someone in my life my own age to share experiences with. Thank you for being there for me, Michael, even if at the time you had no idea what was going on.

I can remember my mother using Mike as a weapon as I got closer to him. Some Parents sometimes say their sixth grader can't go see his buddy, as a punishment for whatever crime he's done, but, again, my mom had to one-up everyone else: she pulled me out of both karate and Boy Scouts as a form of punishment, and, even worse, she told me that Mike would hate me and not play with me anymore if I didn't do such-and-such the way she wanted. To a kid that age, it was a serious threat. I guess that explains why I held on to Mike so tightly as my BFF, and constantly reminded him of that fact. It was borderline smothering, but what's a kid supposed to do? My mother always had such a twisted and conniving way about her, I lived in constant fear of losing what little I had—again.

During that time, I became involved in plenty of extracurricular activities, like fistfighting. Despite my friendship with Mike, I was still the weird kid, and other children my age saw this weakness and took advantage of it. I became close friends again with the principal at my school and spent plenty of time at in-school suspension. Mike and I actually became close friends by getting into one of these face-to-face battles. Funny how it all works out.

I took tae kwon do as a self-defense class, because I was getting my ass beat left and right. I can recall one particular time when a boy at my bus stop hit me hard over the back with a Wiffle-ball bat. It did no damage, but it stung for a while—until I pulled a roundhouse on him (Chuck Norris gave me permission) and he went to the nurse's office at school. I was a hero for one day of my life. Unfortunately, there were still many days to come when kids wanted to help teach me a lesson—the hard way. My parents never did realize that they helped to make me the way that I was, and am, and in turn helped put me in that situation. It is interesting how much you can figure out when you become older and step out of your childhood circumstances.

Even then, I sensed that the older I got, the fewer friends I would have. I finally came to accept the fact and just planned on playing by myself every day. If this was true of you, too, take time to reflect on and remember where you came from. You are *not* to blame for being the "weird" kid at every stage of your life. Abuse can add certain undesirable attributes to a person, and it was not necessarily your fault that you had to suffer through that. Remember the beautiful person that you are, hold on to that, and cherish what is inside you that makes you happy. There is a beautiful you underneath all that has been piled on top of you— find that person and embrace him or her!

Anyway, enough of living in O'Fallon—I was now in seventh grade, which meant it was time to move again. We packed up our brown mobile home and relocated it to some acreage in Troy, Missouri. I loved that piece of land. It was plenty big to escape to, and I was old enough to travel around it safely. My parents bought me a three-wheeler, and I wore a path around the perimeter of the property like an animal in a zoo cage.

Over and over, day after day, I rode that piece of land, taking my pretend friends on tours.

My parents were getting worse again, this time on a whole new level. There used to be some breaks in their arguing, but it had become ridiculous. There were no compliments or love between them—only the brewing rage of an unhappy wife and her husband's defensive actions. My mother complained about everything my father ever did, where we lived, and what he was doing.

I did have another great escape from reality that I worked on tirelessly throughout one lonely summer: my tree house. This thing was awesome! A lift-up STOP sign for a door, real glass windows from an old nearby house, electricity from the shed via extension cords, and many places for me to hide. I spent many nights at this location, listening to the rap-and-R&B radio station the Quiet Storm. This was my getaway my escape from the Trailer of Anger, 250 feet away.

Mike and his family lived only five miles away, but it sure was a long ride there. My dad was always at work, and I could hardly ever get my mother to take me. She was busy doing guess what? Yep, smoking one cigarette after another at the kitchen table. (Hey, we all need some sort of hobby.) But I loved going to play with Mike whenever I got the chance.

I stated earlier that kids sometimes find a person older than they are to look up to and help them solve their problems. This is where my uncle P comes in. He was a great man with whom I could spend hours and share what was happening inside the four walls of my parents' trailer. I'm not sure why my parents trusted him so much, but they let me go anywhere I wanted with him. What a neat man. For the next year or so of my life, I entrusted many secrets to him. I was into karate at the time, and I considered myself the Daniel-san to his Mr. Miyagi.

Unfortunately, my mother introduced Uncle P to one of my aunts on her side, and that was the end of a beautiful relationship for me. This aunt was busy trying to spend what little money Uncle P made and punishing him the way the rest of that side of the family did their spouses. They got married, divorced, and remarried all within a short time.

Then Uncle P and I had a falling-out after something he and my mother supposedly did that was not acceptable and I could not understand. I remember him taking me for a ride in his truck and pulling into the parking lot of a church that my family had attended when I was younger. He then proceeded to play an audiotape that he and my mother made of them having sex, supposedly as a way to make someone he knew jealous. I still don't know if they actually performed the act, but I am sure that it was my mother. I'm also not sure why the hell Uncle P played this tape for me, but I didn't want anything to do with him after that. I still don't get it! And that was the end of P.

This area was also the birthplace of my DJ skills, thanks to two cousins who lived together a few miles down the road. Dylan and Lenny were the cool dudes everyone wanted to hang out with at school. They were mysterious and had a rough relationship with their family as well. (As I've told you, kids often find other kids like them to associate with.) This was a house where I spent many hours after school and honed my DJ skills using rap music and old-school funk. Dylan and Lenny also tried (unsuccessfully) to teach me how to break-dance. We stayed in contact for many years.

I also made some enemies at school around that time. This crew used to pick on me nonstop (remember, kids will look for weaknesses in other kids and expose them quickly), stealing my lunch money, taking my books, and tripping me in the halls. I had originally not planned to publish any names in this book, but the leader of this group of bullies deserves whatever comes his way.

Frank was in the seventh grade, like I was, and he was small, wiry, and mean. He could punch his way through a brick wall (I thought he was Mike Tyson at the time), and the daily ass-beatings he and his friends gave me went on for almost a year. Although I later found out that Frank was physically abused—his father would throw him through windows, break bottles and threaten him with the glass, and so on—this is the only guy I don't really feel sorry for, because he took out all of his poor home life unfairly on me. I'm sure he's following the rules now and beating his own children.

I'll tell ya what, Frank's kids: I'll sell you a copy of this book at half price, to thank your old man for being such a dick! (Just kidding—I hope he's figured his life out. Maybe.)

I finally reached a breaking point in the seventh grade when I knew that I was not really wanted and unloved. At least, I thought it must have been the case, because my parents always told me that. Not only was I nothing but a burden to them, but I had also become the catalyst of all of their problems.

I remember vividly the night I ran away from the trailer: I wrote a note, packed my red-haired toy poodle and her dog dish, and rode the five miles to Mike's home on a busy highway on my moped. It was dark and cold out, but it didn't matter—it was time for me to leave. I had experienced enough at that hell house on wheels!

I still remember the distinct feeling of being unwanted by the two people who were supposed to be there for me through thick and thin. I hated them and myself for what I had done wrong. Oh, wait—I didn't actually do anything wrong to them; they just blamed me for all the problems in their marriage.

I'm not so sure now if I left home to just get away temporarily or for a permanent vacation, but whatever it was, I know I planned on staying gone. I remember pulling out of my driveway in tears because of the pain, but I also had a small lump of pride in my throat, because I knew I was escaping.

When I pulled into Mike's driveway, I was in tears and just wanted a place to stay—somewhere away from what was as close to hell as I could experience at such a young age. I told Mike's mom a bit about what was going on, and then I went to bed. I felt safe in their home and actually felt like someone cared. Remember, Mike was truly my best, and essentially only, friend at the time. No matter what the circumstances, I always felt a sense on love and protection from this family.

But a few hours later, I was rudely awakened. It was sometime around 3:00 or 4:00 AM when my father came to get me. He had to go to work and must have found me missing and read my note about moving away from home. He took me back home, told me essentially that I was a worthless piece of shit for running away, and asked how I could do this to him and my mother. He then went to work—and left me with her. I cannot really recall what else happened that day, but I know that I was blamed for their problems and again all of the blame was placed on me. I was also told what an embarrassment I had caused them for leaving their house of love and all that they had provided for me.

They did not console me. They did not hug me. They did not tell me that everything was going to be okay. They did not apologize. They did not care. They just continued to blame everything on me and tell me what an inconvenience I was to them. This was the morning that I truly remember not loving my parents as much as I could.

My advice to you is to leave the door of communication and love as open as you can for your kids as they grow up. They need you. Listen to them and take a hint; they will help steer you in the right direction. My parents did not listen to me. It hurt like hell then, and, regrettably, it still does to this day.

Chapter 7: Leaving My Father . . . Again?

In this chapter, I will just touch upon my school career and where I am at in my lifeline to give you a point of reference in my life story. Until now, I have written this book in a mostly chronological fashion so you could follow my timeline, but this will be the final chapter that follows that template, as I need to focus on more events and what happened during them. It will be easier to read and understand my story if I pull them into line that way. Some of them may fall on and off of the clock a bit.

My mother and father had a knack for picking the worst time to escalate the problems in their "special" relationship. This time was no different than any other. I felt that I was actually starting to find my place at school, as I had begun taking my musical preferences for rap and R&B to heart. Oprah coined the term "wigger" a couple of years after I perfected my role, but I was a founding father. Adidas high-tops with no shoe laces (RUN-DMC), a Kangol hat (LL

Cool J), brightly colored jogging suits, and a not-too-thick gold chain (I didn't have a job yet) were my wardrobe of choice. I also had the walk down: a little bit of a swagger. Finally, I perfected the talk. This was the most important part: I dropped my hillbilly twang and picked up an overnight course in Ebonics. Watch any given episode of *Jerry Springer*, and you'll get the picture. It was phat, yo!

We gave away the moped and tore down the tree house, and my mother and I moved to the "city" after my parents separated once again. I can't recall what triggered the breakup this time, but it would not be the last. We moved to an apartment in West County, Manchester, Missouri, which was part of the Parkway school district. This was yet another chance for me to start anew, only this time, I had established a bit more of myself and my personality—even if it wasn't the kind any of my fellow students would want to associate with.

This area had an interesting socioeconomic mix of middle-class and upper-middle-class residents. My mother and I didn't live next to the rich people, but we certainly had more class than the "country folk" who had lived next to us in the trailer parks. The St. Louis suburbs were divided demographically into North County, where the population was primarily African American, and South County, which was full of Hoosiers and rednecks. East St. Louis was all hood; same for most of the city. Then there were Ladue and Clayton, which housed the old money in the area. Finally, West County was where the new, young money moved.

St. Louis had a citywide desegregation program that mandated the busing of inner-city kids an hour and a half from their homes to the rich kids' high school. Not the best idea I'd ever heard of—the rich kids marked their territory very well and did almost anything they had to do to protect it, and any wrongdoings at school were always the city kids' fault, at least according to the wealthy students.

The rich kids were the majority at the school; next in line were the desegregation students. I went to high school in the late '80s and early '90s, so we also had a mix of skaters, punks, and stoners. The stoners were the stereotypical crowd that smoked cigarettes and other herbal products and loved Guns N' Roses. The closed-minded, snotty, BMW-driving rich kids wanted nothing to do with me, but I fit right in with the desegregation crowd during my first couple of years of high school. What few friends I did make were from this community. However, because my home life clouded my mind daily with confusion, anger, and hatred, it was hard for me to establish solid relationships at school. I enjoyed my studies, but I hated the free time during lunch and between classes. And I had essentially lost contact with my best friend Mike when we moved, since my mother never wanted to venture back out to the sticks, so I found myself lonely yet again.

The apartment that we lived in had two bedrooms, two bathrooms, and not enough space to escape my mother or her incessant cigarette smoke. It was down the street from a pre–Best Buy store that I frequented; my other favorite hangouts were a Radio Shack a couple of blocks away and a Streetside Records store that I walked to almost every day after school. In those early years of high school, I spent a lot of time walking by myself up and down the busy street near my apartment. Manchester Road had all kinds of great parks, stores, and restaurants, and while I could never afford to buy anything, it gave me something to do and a way to get out of my mother's apartment.

One great part of living in that area was that my sister's family lived not too far away. My mother and I visited them frequently at their new home, only fifteen minutes away. I have already detailed the visits to my sister's house in earlier chapters, and nothing had changed about her family—they were still amazing, as always.

I was fourteen years old when I got my first real paying job, working as a dishwasher at Miss Sheri's Cafeteria on Manchester Road. It was walking distance from my apartment, and I loved it. My boss gave me as many shifts as I wanted, so I worked a lot. I had finally found the freedom that I was searching for, away from the prison of my mother and her smoking. This place was great! I made $3.15 per hour and spent it all on tapes and soon-to-be compact discs. George

Michael's *Faith* and the Bangles' *Different Light* were the first two CDs that I ever purchased.

I made friends with the manager of Miss Sheri's, and he became sort of a father figure to me. I would confide in him about the goings-on at home, and he would listen, as much as a boss could. Nice guy! I even called him Dad later in our relationship, which he didn't appreciate. I was eventually promoted to the title of assistant dishroom supervisor, or ADS (some of the other kids thought it was funny that the acronym also stood for "absolute dumb shit"), and I spent the better part of three years at this fine establishment. I was anointed nightly in Comet, dirty grease, and leftover food the older clients failed to consume.

My father encouraged me to stay with this job as long as I wanted, though he somehow knew I would not want to make Miss Sheri's a career choice. He was right. Thanks for the lesson, Dad! Over the next couple of years, I also worked at McDonald's, Naugles (a division of Del Taco), Long John Silver's, Red Lobster, Wendy's, Lion's Choice, and Kmart. These jobs, followed by my experience as an independent business owner, helped me come to the conclusion that I do a very good job working for myself, under my own supervision, and can usually meet my own expectations. Even though it is scary at times economically, everything works out in the end. I am great at being my own boss.

As you can tell by the large list of businesses, I went from job to job, usually because I was forced to move (i.e., I was fired), but I always found a means of having spending money. And I was very proud of earning that money, because I did it the hard and honest way. Many hours of long labor for piss-poor pay summed up my high school career until senior year, when I started DJ'ing for income.

At school, I tried to fit in with the other crowds and please everybody all of the time. I pretended not to care much about the people who ran over me and my feelings—*Screw them*, I thought—but their actions only made me feel worse, probably as a result of the abuse that I received at home. I was somewhat impervious to their treatment after the severity of abuse that I had to go through every night. This attitude would, unfortunately, stick with me for many years. I was fortunate, however, to form a few key relationships with the opposite sex during my high school career. These young ladies had all come from some sort of broken background, as I had—further supporting my theory that abused children look to form relationships with companions who are similar to them.

And now, here we go again! Somehow, after about six months, my parents decided that their strong and inseparable relationship would make it again if my father moved back in. Whatever. This was actually beneficial for me, though, because we moved to a bigger apartment with a separate downstairs bedroom. Teenage privacy rocks! They actually left me alone for a while when I was working constantly at Miss Sheri's. I think this was because I left immediately after I got home and didn't come in until they were both in bed.

I am not sure how or what or why, but my parents decided to stick together over the next couple of years (sort of) and enjoy each other's company. We bought a house in Ballwin, Missouri, a town adjacent to Manchester. This was the only place we lived that I really loved—although, ironically, it was also the house where the most damage to me would be done.

At first, I continued to do well academically. Besides getting on their every last nerve because of my ADHD, I grew close to many teachers throughout my high school years, some of whom I am still in contact with today. The combination of my abusive home life and the mean, bullying kids at my school was a heavy load to bear, and I truly believe that these gifted individuals kept me going through what was to become the worst part of my life. I was also very close to my high school counselor, Mr. S, whom I saw daily. I told him many secrets about me that I would never reveal to anyone else besides Becky; in return, he became my best friend and worked hard to make sure that I made it through high school. Eventually, he even helped save my life.

Chapter 8: Why Live? Thank You, Jesus!

I remember so many little stories about this portion of my life, my teens, in the late 1980s, and I would love to share them with you. There are many things that I am about to type that I have never told anyone. I am not sure if these memories are so vivid because of my increased awareness as a teenager or because of the horror that I had the pleasure to live every single day. I do know that as I reflect on my past, I can recall a lot of pain, anger, hopelessness, and uncertainty about what was to come. I lived my life day to day, hour to hour. I could not wait for each moment to pass so I could get past whatever was happening during that exact second. I wanted someone to save me, but no one ever did—until what was almost the end.

It was an unusually warm spring or early summer at the end of ninth grade when we moved into a house on Spring Glen Drive. It was a simple, grayish-blue home on a corner lot, with two bedrooms, two bathrooms, and a fireplace in the living room.

There were a few trees, a concrete retaining wall, and a patio out back.

My parents had always kept their living quarters clean, and this place was no exception. The house smelled brand new until my mom and her cigarettes arrived. I loved mowing the lawn there, as it meant I could go outside and breathe in fresh air. To this day, I sleep with a fan blowing directly on my face for this sole purpose.

During this time, I opened up my narrow musical mind and became a huge fan of the Beatles—I mean groupie-fanatic huge. I had always felt that I would have been a better child of the '60s, given my musical tastes and my interest in world peace, though, with my luck, I would have ended up in Vietnam. I can thank Mommy (whom I will write about in a few chapters) for this introduction to "real" music, which I still hold dear to my heart today. I have seen Paul McCartney live almost fifteen times in the past ten years. He is truly the only famous person whom I would love to meet.

Instead of playing with the friends that I did not have outside, I would lie in the dark and listen to Beatles albums over and over and over. Those dudes were deep. Teens who are reading this book: open up your minds beyond all the murder-focused, sexualized hip-hop and synthesized electronica today and listen to something real. Because I'm a DJ by trade, I enjoy that other music, too, but don't close your mind to what your parents and their parents listened to. It may be the only good thing that they can pass on to you.

My sophomore year in school was about to start, and my father and I built a bedroom in the basement for me. I spent most of my time in there, coming out only to eat and go to school. I would have been a fool to sit and watch TV with my parents at night, as I would become even more the object of their anger, an outlet for their problems.

My mother and father had a routine that I became accustomed to during this period of high school. It was quite simple, really: my mother would smoke on the couch in the living room (she had gradually moved from the kitchen table to a lazier place in the house), and my father would work, come home, and then collapse on the floor. This also marked the period when my dad started having heart problems. As much as I would like to blame my mother for them, his genes really sucked.

My schedule became somewhat patterned as well. I would wake up to secondhand smoke, have a bowl of cereal, and hop on the bus. I would then go fearfully into the education building and spend at least half of the day in Mr. S's office. I would finally come home to what I hoped would be an escape from my shitty day, only to find things getting worse.

My parents spent all their free time venting their hatred and disdain toward each other around me. And when they were done blaming each other, they turned their focus to me: "I hate you!" "We would have been much better off if I had that abortion your father wanted." "Why can't you just be normal!" (That last one is kind of a contradiction, isn't it? You want me to be "normal" like the rest of the kids, while neither of you is anywhere close to "normal" yourselves?)

If there ever were any filters in my parents' language, they had disappeared by now. Anytime I tried to communicate with them about any topic, they just told me how little they cared, then hurled a verbal dagger at me—and it cut deep. They told me over and over again during my next semester of school how much I was not wanted, how much they hated me, how they had wished that I had never been born, and also how they could have made that happen via medical procedure. I don't care how tough a person thinks they are—these words and their corresponding nonverbal actions would penetrate deep into anyone's soul. My mother and father together mastered the art of destroying the only living thing that they made together. I felt like nothing—just empty.

This verbal abuse went on for months, and I could do nothing about it. I would just lie in my room and cry and wonder about all of the "whys" that I wrote about in the foreword. No one cared; no one would listen to me; no one was there for me to cry on or get a hug from. Whatever little bit of dignity I'd had, my parents raped from me with their harsh words of hate, and I had had enough.

One rainy night in the late fall of my sophomore year, my parents left home to do some shopping and have dinner. They invited me to go, but I refused this particular evening, as I already had plans. There were no "I love yous" or "Be safes" as they departed—same as it was every other night after we moved into that house. I was sad, lonely, heartbroken, angry, and empty all at the same time. There was nothing left in me. I could not take it anymore. I had no friends, no family, or anyone else (who wasn't paid) to care for me. This was it.

I found my mother's gun in a box under their bed. Besides a BB gun that would "shoot your eye out," I had never held a weapon before. For its size, the brushed-nickel handgun was heavy. I am not sure of the make and model of the weapon, but that did not matter to me at the time—it represented only a tool to end my existence and my pain. As I held it, I was petrified, shaking, and thinking selfish and scared thoughts all at the same time:

This will teach them not to hate me.

This will stop their arguing with each other.

What did I ever do wrong to all of these people for them to hate me so much?

It won't hurt anymore; it will all quietly slip away.

I can still remember the taste of the gun as I put it in my mouth: kind of like an old penny. I sat there for a while, with the gun in my mouth, thinking. Thinking of the "whys" I previously wrote about. Questions that I couldn't even begin to answer were now forming. I couldn't do anything but shake and cry. I just wanted someone, anyone, to help me. And then I began to pray.

"Jesus, please help me. I am so scared, and I don't know what to do. Please help me!"

And then, just like my father at the justice of the peace's altar on his wedding day, I heard a little voice pop into my head. It was quiet and soothing and penetrated the crazy thoughts running through my head.

I am here for you.

Talk about divine intervention. I really felt a presence of peace that I had never felt before come over me. While continuing to sob, I took the gun back to my mother and father's room and gently put it away.

My parents came home that night in the midst of one of their heated discussions, and I interrupted them while they were yelling at each other, by saying something like, "Hello? Hello? Can you stop fucking yelling at each other for a second? I just tried to hurt myself."

Silence. No one came over to hug me or console me. No kind words were said. They just stared at me; their glares almost burned a hole through me. I cannot remember exactly what my mother said, but she aimed words of blame at my father like bullets. What a night.

My father took me to the hospital that my school counselor had mentioned to my mother. He did not say a word of kindness or understanding on that trip. All I remember him saying was that he had to get up and go to work early in the morning. He also mentioned how weak I was for trying to harm myself and our "family."

He checked me into the Weldon Springs Hospital (I told you I would be there sooner or later) and filled out the necessary paperwork. This was a psychological rehab facility, similar to the one my parents met in. It's interesting now to think of the cycle that has happened with my family; it has come full circle. I don't remember my father hugging me or saying any kind words before he left, but I do know he went to work the next day.

I am going to stop for another moment and just pray to God that my daughters and my family never have to go through the pain that I went through. I shouldered this alone, as my parents came to visit only once during my month-long stint in there. Even after something serious like this, they still did not care and certainly were not interested in fixing their relationship with each other, or me. This experience ingrained in me the desire to do my absolute best, as a parent, to be there for both of my little angels, no matter what their needs may be.

During that month. I went to group sessions and art-therapy classes and did my schoolwork; that was about it. In a facility like Weldon Springs, you are under lock and key, with no in-and-out privileges. These places are designed to help "fix" people and their problems and then reintroduce them to the real world. I and the other screwed-up patients were all in there for different reasons, but most of us had tried to end our lives early.

The rehabilitation program was a level-based therapy healing process. You would either advance to the next level or step down a level, depending on how well you did in your counselor's eyes. I can recall thinking that this place was bullshit and that I just needed someone to help me fix my home life. Whatever the case may be, I did happen to get a much-needed break from the hell that I was living at home. It was like a padded-wall vacation.

There *was* one unforgettably funny piece of this whole pie: I was trying to get some sleep on my first night, and every night after, while I was there, but my roommate, Joe, had a bad habit of jerking off before he went to sleep. Great! I was a teenage boy, too, but I had the decency to wait until I was alone, not bop my salami around with another frickin' dude in the room. I asked to be moved out of that room, but no other beds were available, so I had to spend the next month with Joe, the hairy-palmed guy.

My vacation ended abruptly when my parents pulled me out early, which is a therapeutic no-no. My mother and father both picked me up in my father's truck, which had only a front seat. There I was, next to my two least favorite people in the world (at the time, at least—my father's ranking has since improved) and my mother had her cigarette going, as usual. I was crammed into the seat like a sardine. I remember giving my mother a blue-and-pink towel rack that I made her in the psych ward. She pitched it onto the floor. *Here we go*, I thought.

I spent the forty-five-minute ride home in silence. I actually wanted someone to say something, but nothing came out. My mom and dad did not ask how I was, how I had been, or how I was feeling. There was no care or concern, and no talking.

When we pulled into our driveway, I wanted to get out of that truck as soon as I possibly could. It was a short run to the doorway and before they put the keys in the door I yelled at them, "Sorry I was such a fucking inconvenience for the both of you!"

I went inside, turned on the Beatles, turned off the light in my room, and went to bed.

The only thing that I can tell you is that there is *nothing* worth ending your life over. Even though your mind may say different, you are special, important and necessary to this world and to the people around you. Don't ever give up or in. Remember that there are times when you may not see value in yourself, but there is always light at the end of the tunnel. You are worth it! You can and will make it!

Chapter 9: Why Live? Part Two

I can remember going to school the next day and having what seemed like the whole school stare at me, both the teachers and the students. Embarrassing! I am not sure if they knew where I had been over the past few weeks or what I was doing, but they knew I went somewhere. I caught up on my studies rather quickly, and my teachers ended up being extra kind, while most of the kids were still the same selfish assholes driving BMWs Mommy and Daddy had bought for them. Not much had changed since I'd left, but at least it was good to get away from my old roommate at the psych ward, the hairy-palmed masturbator.

You would figure that after such a traumatic family episode, some major positive changes would have taken place at home. Not so. My home life just continued on its usual course and then became even worse. Now, my parents had new weapons to use against me, based on my experiences at the hospital. My father did not dig in as deep as my mother; he usually just complained about the finances involved with my hospital stint. My mother had a knack for using whatever I had said or done wrong in the past as a weapon against me, no matter how badly it would hurt. She could find my weak spots and was willing to expose and exploit them to gain an advantage over any given situation, at any given time.

Abortion was her weapon of choice. As I wrote about earlier, my father sometime during my mother's pregnancy must have considered what torment I was going to go through for the next forty years of my life and must have mentioned it to my mother. My presence on Earth is evidence that his suggestion did not come to fruition, because I am here—and all kinds of screwed up from it, too. No one should *ever* use that discussion as a weapon to instigate fights and manipulate people, but my mother used it daily as a way to put me in my place, to get back at me for saying something out of line, or just to be downright nasty.

I did learn in the psych ward that I should be able to have open communication with my parents about any given topic, so I tested out this idea. I remember talking to my mother about some of the kids bullying me at school, and somewhere along the line the communication took a turn away from the psych-ward textbook and headed south. I am not sure why, but I told her that I was displeased with the way that she carried out some form of parenting and tried to give her input from my point of view. She immediately jumped on the abortion bandwagon and blamed anything and everything on my father.

"Your father wanted me to have an abortion, but I carried you and raised you all alone. He was never there for you, and I did everything."

No matter what the topic, my mother would always blame my father for anything and everything that did not happen in her favor. Then she would rant and rave about how she raised me and did all of the parenting, and how he was a good for nothing so-and-so. (See chapter 4.) In my mother's eyes, she was perfect and innocent and all was great . . . and my father was the devil. I happen to disagree. My father may not have made the top five, but at least he was not just inherently mean.

As I have already stated and you may have guessed, home life just got worse. How does one experience go from bad to worse? It's simple: take a psychotic, prescription medicine–abusing schizophrenic with bipolar disorder and add an enabler to the mix, and there you have it—instant hell! Remember, as I got older, my father's main fault is that he kept throwing me back into the hell, defending the meanness, and not removing me from the situation.

The title of this chapter must give you some indication of where I was heading. Yep, I figured life was not worth living again, so I might as well end it. Only this time I did not insert a gun into my mouth or cut my wrists or do anything to hurt myself. I just wanted life to be over. I had reached my breaking point all over again, all within the same year. In fact, I wanted to die so badly that I actually asked my father to take me to the hospital again.

Dad: "You don't need no hospital. Grow up and get over it! Tough it out!"

Me: "But I'm really scared, and I don't want what happened last time to happen again."

Dad: "That hospital bill's going to be thousands of dollars."

Me: "Don't we have insurance for this stuff?"

Anyway, we loaded up the car and I moved to the quack house again (said to the tune of *The Beverly Hillbillies*). I really don't think my parents ever knew the form of tool that I tried the first time to rid the earth of one more asshole, but I'm guessing they do now.

This time, my experience at the hospital was a little different. The hospital staff warmly welcomed me back, because they remembered my being there less than a year earlier. I did not have a monkey-spanking roommate; it was just me in my room. It was pretty empty in the hospital, compared with the time before. (I guess I was good for business.)

The only problem is that my parents really did not believe in this program. My mother just continued her mean streak and threw out countless invalid insults at me to undermine any of the slight progress I was making. My father would complain about the finances and would say how useless these "quacks" were and how "you ain't gonna get any better in this psych ward."

My stay lasted only a week this time. Remember, this was a one- to two-month program designed to help people through some really serious shit—like wanting to end their life early, but my parents pulled me out after an argument that they and I got into with one of the guards.

My sister, her husband, and my parents all came to visit after I had been there a full week. That's a long wait to see your kid in the hospital, if you ask me, especially because the hospital had visiting hours daily. Still, I was actually glad to see everyone. The only problem was, my sister was the only one that believed in this program and believed that I truly had a reason to be in there. (Thanks, Sis!)

We sat down for lunch, and all hell broke loose. My mother sat and blamed my father, my father complained about the money that it was costing, and my sister was caught in the middle of all this bullshit. I couldn't do much more than sit at the corner of the table and cry. I did pipe up a couple of times, though.

Me: "I do not want to go back home yet. I don't feel safe there and am not ready. I need to finish this!"

Dad: "Cheap! Cheap!"

Mom: "It's your father's fault!"

I responded, "No, this is mainly your fault because you are such a bitch to me and my father! You cause most of my problems! Your hate penetrates me!"

That is the first real time that I can remember speaking up directly to my mother and telling her how I felt. I may not have done it the right way, but it was healthy for me to let her know how out loud I felt. Both of my parents were guilty for various crimes against me, but my mother was, again, the worst.

One of the guards decided he had had enough of the yelling and cursing in his dining room and said it was time for everyone to leave. My father and sister went into the locked-down part of the facility to bring me some clean underwear or something, and my mother went to get her nicotine fix. My sister and father headed down the hall with me, and, unfortunately for me, I just lost it. It was not the best idea, but I could not believe what had just happened. I was not a happy little buddy.

I started yelling and carrying on—nothing physical, just verbal and emotional. I just couldn't take it anymore. *No one actually visited for my benefit (except my sis); you just came here to make my life more uncomfortable. I haven't seen you in a week, and you guys won't even support me; you just wanted to start some shit and leave. Fuck that!*

I yelled, screamed, and disobeyed the guard's instructions to calm down. Have you ever been so angry that you just can't control yourself? That's where I was. Well, after many warnings, I guess it was time for me to kiss the floor. Two security guards got on top of me, and they were not the small kind.

My father was not very happy with this situation and told them to get off his son. I cannot remember all of the words that took place verbatim, but what I do remember is my father throwing two guards down the hall, grabbing my shit, and getting the hell out of Dodge. My father informed the nurses' desk that we were leaving, and we headed for the door. The hospital could say nothing about it, because it was a voluntary check-in in the first place.

We made it outside, and I clearly remember my father saying to my mother, "Put out the damn cigarette—we're going home. No one is going to jump on top of my son!"

Wow! For the first time, I felt some sort of love, care, and protection from him.

I was very excited to go home with my father and his newfound need for protecting me. Even if it was only for a few moments, I felt some sort of umbrella over me. My mother had no idea what just happened. My sister just left with her husband, and that was about it.

The only bad part of all of this is that I did not finish the program and get the help that I truly needed. When you enroll in this type of therapy, you are expected to give it your all and complete the program. Not so for me, and this was the second time that I had left early. In retrospect, I wish my parents had let the professionals do their job. Oh well, I would figure it out.

I did gain some confidence and a new attitude through all of this. I am not sure if it was the therapy itself or all of the excitement surrounding my parents' visit, but that was the last time I ever thought about death as an answer to my problems. Now I would stand up for myself! Now I would speak out my feelings! Now I would not tolerate any one else's shit! I had had enough and was not going to put up with any more abuse! Now I would head down the road of becoming more like my parents . . . Oh, shit!

My newfound emotional freedom was good, until I started to become abusive myself. Now that I am older, I can actually pin to this particular moment the start of the asshole I was about to become. I truly wish that things had gone differently. My friends and family did not deserve the way I began to treat them.

I will now reiterate my thoughts on hurting yourself in any way. It is simply not worth it. There is nothing worth it. Even though *you* may feel like you have little or no value to anyone else in the world, including yourself, you are worth it all. Ending your life is not a way to end the problem. Don't let them win. Face the problem, grasp it with both hands and overcome.

One other note: Don't ever feel like you have to go at this alone. If you need help, ask. People are here for you. Go to my website and you will find some phone numbers. Tell someone. Don't try to tackle the mountain alone. When it is all through, you will truly understand that it was all not as bad as you thought. Don't be afraid or embarrassed to ask someone for help.

Finally, if you enroll in a professional program or seek psychological counseling, stick with it. There is something in your life that has brought you to a point where you feel like you are not worth it, so now get help to find your true value and place in the world. The people there are there for one reason, and that is you.

No matter how bad it may seem, there is hope and there is help. Now, go overcome!

Chapter 10: Broken Girlfriends

I truly believe that a person can and will sniff out friends and lovers that are like them. They will look for someone with the same values, principles, thought process, and will actually share some of the same experiences from the past and maybe even have the same tastes for what is to come for the future. This is most certainly the story in my lifetime, as I had found two long-standing relationships in high school with girls who were in some way like me. Poor things.

I will opt to keep their names sacred, just as I am about to reveal a lot of details that most people besides us don't know. My wife is going to tell me to remove this detail and that story, but I will reveal a lot about myself this way, and you may even get a laugh out of it.

I would like my male readers to pay close attention to some of these details; you will know which ones. If you find a characteristic that is comparable to you and you have had a similar experience, stop now, grow up, and quit being an asshole! I understand what it's like—I was there, brother!

If you are female, then please read on as well. For the women reading this book, if you find that you are in a relationship with someone like the former me, then get out of your relationship now! No one, and I repeat no one, needs to be stuck in a dead-end, controlling, and abusive relationship. It is not your fault that this person is the way he is, and you are not responsible for his problems, so don't try to solve them—it's way too much work. Tell them to get him counseling and then have him look you up on Facebook in three or four years. I know all of this because I was that guy. (And thanks for hanging in there with me, Becky.)

Girlfriend Number One (I'll call her G1 from here on out) came from a broken family. I didn't see any signs of abuse, but she was broken. Her experiences were quite different from mine, as her parents actually got a divorce, instead of tormenting the kids with their issues. She, like my wife, was adopted. I am not sure what any of you knows about adoption, but it is a very expensive process that involves dedication, determination, and a whole lot of love.

It is a different kind of love, though, in the fact that mommies and daddies don't get the privilege of holding their baby at birth and instantly developing that bond with their child. They usually get to meet their loved one a little later in life, after some heavy-duty paperwork and a lot of money is paid. But then it happens. I think that sometimes love from adopted parents may even be a little deeper because those parents had to work their ass off to earn the right to receive that bundle of joy.

I know that this is out of the story line, but it seems to fit. My mother-in-law has told me many times through the rearing of my girls that you do not need a license to raise a child. Think about that for a minute. You need one to drive a car and even one to get married, but with the most precious thing that you can do, all you have to do is procreate. Wow! Hey, I gave my wife the best thirty-two seconds she has ever experienced—twice!

As Snoop Dogg would say, "Back to the lecture at hand." G1's parents spent the first couple of years of her life together and then split it up, which was healthy in one way but also hard for G1, because her parental roots and foundation were now divided. I never did ask the details of why they split, but judging from G1's mom (with whom G1 and her brother lived), I think they just grew apart. Hey, stuff happens, and love and marriage are no exception. At least they made a decision and stuck with it, instead of dragging their children through the hell of uncertainty.

I have said in previous chapters that abuse is passed on from generation to generation and person to person (i.e., shit rolls downhill). Well, G1 was lucky, as we were together when I was in ninth grade, before things got *really* bad. Girlfriend Number Two (G2) got the shit end of the stick.

G1 and I spent a great amount of time together, going to Six Flags, homecoming dances, parades, and dinner, having two-hour make-out sessions (I hope my daughters don't ever read this chapter). I even got to know her grandparents, two of the smartest people I will ever meet. As this was my first real romantic relationship, it was a truly wonderful experience.

I am telling you this story for one reason: it served as a breath of fresh air (literally) from the bullshit that was mounting at home. I don't remember sharing too many details about my family with G1, but I now understand why I clung to friends and girlfriends so strongly and quickly. I used those people as a safety net to protect me from my home life and to replace what I was missing in my own family. Because I didn't have many connections, when I did find someone, I would grasp with both hands and embrace them fully, at times to the point of figurative relationship suffocation.

I am still in contact with G1 and her family off and on to this day. Her mother and I developed a special relationship; I confided in her over the years about my parents, and she became an incredible shoulder to cry on. I owe her a debt of gratitude and truly doubt I could ever repay her for the countless hours that she spent taking care of this extra son, even after G1 and I called it quits. Thank you, Mommy. G1 was my first true love, although I didn't really know it at the time. Also, Mommy was the one who introduced me to the Beatles. (Thank you for that! Love you!)

My story with G2 takes place after my two unsuccessful suicide attempts at home and before my first semester of college. This young lady was stunning, had an incredible personality, and always made me smile. This was the late '80s and early '90s, so she had hair that towered over me, along with a great figure and the cutest laugh I have ever heard. Memories!

G2 was as sweet as they came when I met her, innocent and curious, as most all girls are at that age. She was a Catholic schoolgirl, which meant two wonderful things: plaid skirts with easy access, and hot friends with plaid skirts with easy access. So, how about a sex story? (Subliminal message: *Buy another copy of this book!*) Here we go! Let's tell it as a baseball play-by-play: I was at a home (mine) game with G2. The owners (my parents) were not there. She was frickin' hot! We had three men on the field, and the bases were loaded. I had made it all the way to third base, and I was about to make a steal and slide into home base (yeah for me!). I had my trusty wooden bat, and wham! Three forms of rubber protection later, I made it and scored a run! (Wasn't that hot?)

By the way, I do need to explain one of these details a little more so you girls out there don't start calling out to the man of your dreams. That was three condoms for one session, not three sessions—we were scared as shit! It was the first time for both of us. Sorry to burst the Fabio, Tom Cruise, and Brad Pitt dream you were having—it was just skinny ol' me.

Despite the fact that things were going from bad to worse for me at home, I now, fortunately or unfortunately, had someone to share everything with. G2's family was most definitely broken as well. Her parents had difficulties like everyone else, and I witnessed them arguing a lot. Her parents yelled a lot at each other and their kids. There were two brothers, and G2 was in the middle. The older one absolutely hated me, while the one ending up following somewhat in my career path.

Although I was as skinny as a board, unattractive, with braces and no big muscles to show off to the girls, I was a pure gentleman and a romantic at heart, outgoing and a lot of fun to be with—that is, until I developed an unstoppable and insatiable taste for abusive behavior and became controlling, jealous, and mean. At that time, I did not have any children to share my behavior with, but I became what my parents were bound to turn me into. I was too young to realize it at the time, but I became them—the same way, as I have said before, you will pass on your abusive traits to your own children if you can't stop the cycle.

G2 and I did normal teen things, like going to the movies, walking around the mall, having picnics, eating cheap dinners, and making out, but we also fought a lot. Though that last detail may seem not to fit, we were two very strong and dynamic personalities put together, and both of us came from houses of anger, so it was only natural that we would argue constantly.

There are countless stories that I could tell to help paint this picture, but they all have the same middle and end. We would get into an argument over something seemingly unarguable, we would yell at each other and try to resolve said stupid topic, and then I would become abusive. I wasn't physical with G2, but I was a verbally abusive piece of shit. If I did become physical, it was usually on someone else's public property, breaking their stuff.

I had done it! I had become just like my parents! Anytime something did not go my way, I would attack G2 and say stuff that no one should say to anyone they care about. My verbal knives had nothing to do with the topic at hand; they were just meant to destroy her where it would hurt the most and help her build up a wall against me. After the dust had settled, I would feel bad and try to make up for not only the argument at hand but also the abusive slander that I spouted at the same time.

The worst part of all of this was that shit did roll downhill, and she was the one to catch it! Over time, the innocent and sweet little girl that I met became like me. She would learn not only to react with anger at me for whatever the argument was about, but also to throw weapons of her own that cut deep. I take the sole blame for this undesirable change in her young life and attitude. G2, I am so sorry for what I did wrong to you. You did not deserve it, and I wish I could take it all back.

Her parents must have seen this side of me on more than one occasion. They could see right through me. I am not sure if it was because they could identify with the abuse themselves or because I was just that transparent an asshole. I know that G2 should have listened to them and dumped me, when she could have gotten out easily. But love—and abuse—had already set in.

Remember this, girls and boys: if you are in a relationship now, or in the future, with someone like I have described—someone controlling, mean, jealous and abusive—get out! Once again, it is not your responsibility to fix your abuser and try to make his or her life better. It is not worth all of the agony you are going through to make your love work. Love should just happen; it should not be a career of anger that you have to spend your precious time deliberating.

The formula for abuse and manipulation is simple: after a while in your relationship, your significant other will blame you for all of his or her problems and then strike out against you with other unneeded weapons to make you either feel sorry for that person or to try to get to you on a deeper level. You will then feel like pure shit and will begin to build a wall of protection around yourself to save what little your partner has left of the original you. Your partner will then try to break down that wall to try to fix everything, only to destroy you more in the end. Finally, you will let the wall go and start to believe that your partner is right, true, and just in what he or she said in the first place. This is the part where you will lose yourself and become someone you were not originally intended to be. I write this formula from experience. Trust me, it works the same for everyone. Now, get the fuck out!

But for G2, it was already too late. I had become a master at making her believe in what I was selling, that this was the way things should be. Seasoned abusers often have a hidden talent for seeing a weakness in another person, clamping on to it, exploiting it, and then destroying (maybe quickly, maybe over a long time) their victim. Please know that I am telling you these stories and putting my thoughts in the world to help you identify someone like I used to be so you can save yourself and become a better you.

On many occasions at the start of our relationship, G2 had the pleasure of meeting my mother and father. They were somewhat cordial to the girlfriends I brought to my house but did not ever try to welcome them warmly. They also never tried to hide their abusive attitudes toward me, and eventually toward that other person in my life. My friends, relatives, and former girlfriends were all very familiar with the way my parents operated and usually had no desire to come back to *mi casa* for another visit.

One day, my mother was on one of her angry streaks, for whatever reason, and was being her usual unpleasant self. G2 and I were attending a formal dance that night, and I picked her up and brought her to my house first, at my parents' request, so they could take pictures of us. But when we arrived and interrupted my mother in the middle of one of her great smoke-a-thons, boy, was she pissed about something. She told "the slut" (G2) how "slutty" she looked and started attacking G2's family, accusing them of being from "the wrong side of the tracks." G2 kept her mouth shut, started crying, and headed for the car. I, on the other hand, tried to reason with the psycho (my mother), which was a big mistake.

My mother then walked across the yard toward my car (a silver 1979 Mustang) and continued attacking G2 and her family. She was loud and mean! G2 did not know how to respond, except to try to roll up her window. The whole time, I was outside the car. I had not yet fully developed my big, round, hairy, defensive balls toward my mom yet, as I would soon enough, so I still thought I might be able reason with her, which was insane. (Google the definition of "insane.")

As G2 was rolling up her window, my mother got physical and slapped her in the face, pulled her hair, verbally attacked her . . . you get the point. Not a desirable way to start off a formal dance. G2 got the window up, I got into the car, and we got the fuck out.

You may be wondering what G2 and I did to trigger my loving mother's anger. Not a damn thing—we walked right into it! Regardless, it would not have mattered even if we had done something to set her off, as there is no excusable reason for something like this to ever have happened.

Of course, this wasn't even the end of the story. There became a rule from my mother that I could not call G2 from my parents' house. This was unfortunate, because it was winter. I would have to drive about fifteen minutes in freezing temperatures to the nearest pay phone and take a lot of quarters with me. Still, I would call G2 nightly and talk about teen stuff.

Sometime around then, my parents also kicked me out of the house. I was actually relieved, to some extent, to go live with a buddy of mine in his basement. Anything would have been better than living in that angry house I came from.

Anyway, I could write story after story about other, similar incidents that, but I believe you get the picture: It was not good! My parents were abusive to me, I became abusive to G2, and she in turn followed the same direction. Poor thing. Fortunately, G2 has since become an incredible mother of three and found herself a much more stable and less abusive man.

When I finally graduated from high school, the only people to witness this proud moment were my father and G2. You won't believe this, but my parents were living separately again, although this time, I was living with my father. My mother was angry at my father and me, so she opted not to come to my high school graduation. She would later blame this on her back problem, but she is too shallow and I am too smart to believe that. She just wanted to be a bitch again and prove her point. It hurt—mission accomplished. Still, I thought I had made it. A new chapter in my life was beginning, and I could not wait to get there.

I will summarize this chapter by reiterating an earlier piece of advice: Do not let the shit roll downhill. Do not pass on the cycle of abuse to the others around you. Do not destroy their lives as well.

Tell someone the situation that you are in, and get some help. As I have said before, doing so is not a sign of weakness; it is a move in the right direction. You are never too young or too old to put an end to this cycle—just do it now!

Chapter 11: Freedom: College and My First Wife

You would think that once I got out of the house, everything would have been better, all of my problems would have gone away, and I would have had the fresh start I craved. That is somewhat true, but my parents had special powers. They were magic! Even four hours away, at the other end of the state, their abuse still had an effect on me. Let's explore their magnificence together, shall we?

My father's and my relationship had gotten better over the past couple of years. Moving in with him during my parents' last separation had made for a much better living experience for both of us. I was right in the middle of my senior year of high school when we moved in together and became buddies. Over this six-month stint, I learned that my parents did much better without each other to feed off of—especially my father. He was a whole different man, and parent, from the one I had known at the Spring Glen house. This proved to me that my mother served as a strong catalyst for igniting my father's flames of abuse.

G2 and I had decided that we would stay "together forever," and I gave her a promise ring at my senior prom. Cute, huh? But we made it through only a couple of months of my first year of college before we called it quits, for two reasons: our long-distance relationship, and hot college chicks.

It's funny when I reflect by opening up my senior yearbook every once in a while. Everyone wished G2 and me good luck on getting married and our long, promising future together. (Ah, youth and naïveté.) But three years was a long time to endure with my family. I wish her nothing but the best of luck. Thank you, G2, for all that you gave me.

I had by now moved into the dorms down at a state school in Missouri, known not as much for its academics as for its focus on celebrating. With a mule for a mascot, CMSU was most certainly a party school that I endured for a short while. My major reason for picking this school was a radio broadcast program that I was interest in, but soon discovered the true meaning of working at a public station: NPR—No Personality Radio. For the record, NPR does a great job of providing the news, but it just wasn't for me.

College was fun! I excelled in everything except for math, and I started my company down there and DJ'd a lot of house parties, fraternity and sorority social mixers, and formals. It was a good way to make beer money, and then some. I also found out that this was an excellent way to meet people of the opposite sex.

Even though I was four hours away, my parents still had an impact on my life, especially my mother. She knew exactly what to say that would influence me and change my direction during my early college career; she always had a knack for destroying something good! I finally and thankfully figured out how to hang up the telephone and end the conversation abruptly. Many nights my thoughts were filled with tears and later became drowned in my beers. (Sounds a bit like a country song, doesn't it? Thanks, Hank!)

I spent only a short time at this school, because I could not find a real academic fit and the town,

Warrensburg, was a shithole. There was a Walmart, an Aldi store, and a lot of bars, and the atmosphere was just too dreary and too small town–like for me. So I applied for bigger and better things and transferred to Springfield, Missouri, home of Southwest Missouri State University, whose mascot was a bear. Now, *this* was a real school. People were just a bit more sophisticated, and I felt much more at home. Springfield was a decent-size city, right in the center of the Bible Belt; in fact, it was probably at the buckle. Branson was only forty-five minutes away. Springfield also had the highest number of Chinese restaurants per capita in the United States: the birthplace of cashew chicken. Great little city!

I restarted my company there and picked up the name that has stuck with it for almost twenty-five years now. DJ'ing was a novelty back then; I alternated between CDs and vinyl and soon became popular on my campus for entertaining guests at parties. I also learned to pick up a microphone, and that people in my audiences loved personal interaction.

It's funny how some things never change but only evolve.

I did great in school, except in math (failed again!). I switched majors and focused on marketing and organizational communications, and I changed TV/radio broadcasting to my minor focus. Hey, I even graduated in five years!

SMSU was also where I would find some of my best friends. Chris, S1, P, Cali, and Steve brought years of laughter, and some frustration, to my life. There were always pranks being played, memories to be made, drinks to enjoy, and fun to be had. I could tell a lot of good stories because of these people in my life, but one of them is a politician, so I'd better keep my mouth shut about most of them.

However, the following story makes me smile to this day. S1 made Chris and me brownies as a treat out of the blue. Unbeknownst to me, she made two separate pans for her two favorite boys in the world . . . only one was a little different than the other. I remember saying to Chris that these things tasted a little weird, and we both agreed that we did not want to hurt her feelings, so we finished half a pan each. Not such a great idea!

My pan was tainted with a tasty laxative, and I had to DJ that night. Thankfully, I had Meatloaf's "Paradise by the Dashboard Light" cued up to excuse myself with. *Dumb and Dumber*–level pain was setting in (you know the scene). It was a long and exciting night! Many trips to the bathroom later, I finally made it to the safety of my dorm. I did retaliate, by putting Icy Hot in S1's panties one night before she had a hot date. Vengeance was mine!

While my life was finally taking a turn for the better, my parents remained the same and continued down their path. I nearly halted all communications with my mother and finally developed a sense of confidence that I had never had before. I didn't really analyze my abuse too much in college, as I was busy studying, getting drunk, and hanging out with friends. None of them really knows this, but all these people served as a much-needed break for me from my parents' daily abuse. Thank you, guys—you saved my life!

I found my first wife in a store in St. Louis, when I went home on a holiday break from school. She was climbing on a ladder, looked down and slipped off, and I was there to catch her. Talk about falling in love! Wife Number One (W1) was a supercute brunette with long, curly hair, a cute ass, and baby teeth. She was one of the most considerate and sweet people I have ever met.

W1 also came from an abusive household with some screwed-up parents. These people barely held on to jobs, smoked a lot of weed, and did a shitty job at raising their kids. I am not sure if they were the mean, abusive type, like my parents, but they were less than impressive. I am simply amazed that this girl came from that environment. Again, poor thing.

She was a beautiful girl and was very sweet but lacked self-confidence, as evidenced by her choice in careers, her lack of focus and determination, and her decision to marry me. When I met her, there was not an angry or mean bone in her body—she was just not built that way. But after time, and abuse from me, all of that changed, and she became, unfortunately, just like me. I didn't understand how all of this worked until I read *Toxic Parents*; then it clicked. I am sorry, W1, for the abuse that I brought into your life. You did not deserve it!

We dated for about three years, and the overall abuse would take its toll on our relationship as we went down the road. And, of course, the best solution to a problem is to add another problem to it—so we decided to get married. No one was pregnant, no one was forcing us; it was just a stupid answer to a hard question. We figured that if we got married, things would settle down and become all the better. Not true!

W1 and I used to argue over every little thing that we could possibly argue about. You name it, we fought about it. This pattern, of course, stemmed from the angry and hostile attitude that I brought in as my gift to our growing love life. We were always on edge with each other over the smallest things but at the same time were very much in love. The good times usually outweighed the bad, so we figured we had a chance at making it work.

Unfortunately, the scenario would turn out the same as my prior relationships, with an added twist. It seemed like I had learned not only how to abuse someone but to be mean to her as well. I know these traits seem repetitive, but there is a difference. You don't necessarily have to be mean to be an abuser. There are different types and levels of abuse. Well, I was both and then added the icing on the cake: control. I was a controlling asshole that demanded my hands in every decision and activity that she tried to do.

This was something a bit new to me because my previous relationships were with stronger females. This is not to say anything bad about W1; she had just not been put in a situation before where she needed to exert any strength. I saw this open door and walked right through it, by trying to control every aspect of her life. I would also become angry and mean if my controlling efforts did not go the way I wanted them to. So now my circle was complete: abuse, meanness, anger, and control.

Let me again point out that these relationships that I shared with the women in my life all seemed to extend from the same formula. I would somehow find an attractive, but not particularly self-confident, mate and reel her in. We would do great in the beginning together, and then, as couples do as they grow, we would find things that were different about each other. Here is where the problems would start. I, like my mother, would seek out and exploit these differences, would not always win, and would become abusive if I did not. No one is perfect, but I will accept the responsibility for destroying these relationships and scarring these girls. Verbal abuse—or any other type of abuse—does not just stop when the abuser leaves the abused. The repercussions carry on for a long time after all is said and done, until both parties stop the cycle themselves.

I have not mentioned much of my parents in this chapter because for the most part, they were out of my life. I had weekly conversations with my mother and usually ended up hanging up on her or cutting the conversation as short as I could. My father and I would talk a bit more often than that. I would still head home to spend the holidays and some of the summer breaks with them. My parents had done their job, accomplished their tasks, and completed their mission. They had completely fucked up their only offspring together and created an exact replica to follow in their footsteps and carry on the cycle of abuse. Congratu-fucking-lations!

Time after time, I would try to figure out what was really wrong with me and why I was the way I was, but I never could. This revelation would not come until later in my life, when I was married to my beautiful current wife and she helped me to see how my abuse was affecting her and my child. I will elaborate more on her in a few chapters. But first, I've got some more wacko shit to talk about!

When I graduated college, I packed up my stuff and headed to Seattle, where W1 was living at the time. She had joined the navy a few years prior and was finishing her service call. We were married three months before I actually moved up to the great Northwest, and we made it another five months while I was up there. During those eight long months, there were good times and bad, but the latter definitely won the prize.

Although we mostly fought, Seattle was beautiful, even though it rained a lot. This was certainly a God-given, tree-hugging part of the country, and W1 and I enjoyed that much together. We had a great little apartment that was situated in a dense forest, had a hot tub, and was only minutes from everything. To this day, it is my favorite home I've ever lived in.

Unfortunately, things inside the walls were not so great. Besides our nonstop arguing, W1 was diagnosed with obsessive-compulsive disorder (OCD), which pretty much took over her life. It controlled her every movement and thought and really took a toll on our relationship. This diagnosis, along with my verbal and emotional abuse, served as a catalyst to intensify the already rocky road that we were traveling.

On Mother's Day in 1996, I called it quits. We rolled over in bed to face each other, and I told her that I had had enough. At the time, it was a hard and mean decision, but I am glad for the both of us that I made it.

Unfortunately, I was in no place to properly care for her newfound situation (the OCD) and manage my own fucked-up life as well. W1 deserved better than what I could give her.

Please keep in mind that I still had not reached a point of where I understood that I was the main instigator in all of these abusive relationships that I have written about. I typically blamed my partners for all of our problems, no matter who was at fault. This is a key point to note and remember as you finish the rest of this book, as I would not figure it all out until five years into my next marriage. Back then, I was just an abusive asshole who would blame everyone else and then add fuel to the fire. Armed with the great education my parents gave me, I would over and over destroy lives and relationships as I moved forward.

Maybe it is because I became so blinded in the heat of the moment in these arguments that all I could do was blame the other person. Maybe it was the anger that took its course of action on me and the other person. Or maybe it was my own physical and emotional scars that made my life so difficult, even though that was the only way I knew to act. Whatever the final facts are, I was destroyed and kept the cycle of abuse alive as I continued down the road toward becoming more and more like my parents.

You might be in the same boat, unable to see or understand the problems and difficulties that you have been through, are going through, and are going to continue to go through. This is very typical of the cycle of abuse. You must identify who you are, what is going on in your life, and where your problems came from in the first place. Then and only then can you begin your journey to making a better you for yourself and everyone around you. It will be hard work, but the benefits completely outweigh the losses in this battle.

Start now by identifying the abuser that you are and where it all came from. Feel free to be angry at what you have become. You were not born that way and did not deserve what has happened to you. But you *are* responsible for you now, and for ending what has been passed on to you. Start now and make a change.

Chapter 12: Sue You, Family!

My soon-to-be-ex-wife and I loaded up our truck and moved back to St. Louis. A couple of good things actually did come of this permanent separation. First and foremost, we have remained friends to this day. I can't say that she was not angry with me over what happened, but in the end we realized that it was best for both of us. Second, we didn't have any children together. My life would be completely different now if that had been the case. Neither of us would have been prepared for that kind of shock to our relationship. Finally, we were broke and didn't own anything/owe shit to hardly anyone. I gave her the car, dishes, and bed and kept my DJ stuff. All was good.

I am not sure if any of you readers have been in a situation like this, but there does, sooner or later, come a downside to all of this fun. Regardless of the situation, circumstances, or timing, you still got married for one reason or another. But in the course of a permanent separation, you lose your mate who you thought would be your lifelong partner. You will also miss that person and their camaraderie, no matter what kind of disagreements you had during the course of your relationship. It's never a complete win-win during any kind of separation. I would know—my parents have proven this theory with great frequency.

I made the mistake of moving back home with my parents for about a month and a half. Things were pretty much the same as when I had left before college. My mother was toking away on a smokestick on the couch day after day, and my father was tolerating her abuse. After having been on the outside of all of it for a while, I realized it was quite evident where the abuse stemmed from. This is not to say that my father was innocent of said charges, but he would usually retaliate against the problems that were presented before him. Simply put, he had mellowed out some and she'd just gotten worse. Welcome home!

It was a quick stay, but I had to get out, make a living, and get away from my parents' unhealthy roof. As an entertainer, I was interested in the cruise-ship industry and thought a six-month contract, a roof (or something like that) over my head, and plenty of women to play with sounded like the perfect getaway formula.

I started on a top-notch cruise line, with a six-month contract in Alaska, on one of the nicest ships at sea, which could hold about two thousand passengers and one thousand crew members. This was not one of the gigantic vessels of today, with an onboard ice rink and a shopping mall; it was much more quaint. And it was an unmatched experience that I will never forget.

Let me paint a picture for you of life on a cruise ship so you can continue to visualize my life span. Cruising is an adventure that you develop a taste for. Once you get that first bite, you will want to do it over and over again; my family and I still cruise frequently as passengers. When I was an employee, the sights, food, and fun were awesome, but they did become a bit stale after the first half of a contract was up. My cruise family—the officers, staff, and crew—were from over one hundred different countries, so a lot of diversity was to be had. It never really felt like culture shock for me, thought, because I was so excited to meet people from different places.

The only part that really ground on me was the repetitive schedule of day-after-day life on the ships. The grind was the same, always. I was also always on the clock. If a passenger approached me during my well-deserved time off the ship, I still had to entertain that guest and represent the company. I was never off-stage—which would prove invaluable for my future in the entertainment industry. Practice makes perfect!

Then there were the Greeks! I have a feeling if my book is distributed internationally, I will sell the shit out of it in this wonderful country. The next statement is not intended to be biased or judgmental; in fact, if you are Greek, you will most likely agree. As a whole, Greeks are loud and controlling in any given situation, and anger easily if they do not get their way. Not to say that they are not nice people, but there is a stereotype of cruise-ship officers that they fulfill.

I was treated as royalty because of my job description, and because I was one of only a handful of US citizens working on the ship. Everyone wanted to be the DJ's friend because I could provide the closest thing to reality that the employees could grasp: music. No matter what reason you have for working on a ship—money, independence, or just to get away—you always miss reality.

Back in the late 1990s, things like cell phones and email were not as widely used and available as they are these days. Communication was much different, even that short a time ago. I contacted my friends and family as often as I could in port, to find out what was going on back in the real world. As you spend time on the ships, you start to lose touch with reality, so any contact is good contact. Yes, I even called my parents a couple of times a week to say hello. Have no fear—same shit.

One particular time when I called home proved to be special on my sliding scale of memories. I called to chat with my father, and he was home, as I had expected. But something was wrong when I spoke with him. My mother, who was supposed to be in Arizona, visiting my sister and her family, was home early. I remember vividly saying to my mother when she picked up the phone, "What did you do this time?"

The conversation continued, "I'm gonna sue your sister for all that money she stole!"

"I'm quite sure you gave it to her to keep for you and forgot about it," I said.

"I ain't crazy, and I don't forget anything. She stole it! She's going to hell!" [*Puff, puff, smoke, smoke.*]

What really happened was that my mother's paranoia got to her, and she started some shit with my sister and her family at her house in Arizona. Nice. Now she had lost all communication with her only daughter, her son-in-law, and her two grandsons.

My mother accumulated her funds from a small allowance from my father, a couple of home sales, and a bunch of lawsuits that she had won using the poor-me card. She was an amazing saver and had a knack for turning a penny into a dollar rather quickly.

My mother had undoubtedly given my sister a great portion of her funds to keep them away from my father and had either forgotten the amount of the donation or forgotten the whole concept altogether. Don't forget, my mother is always right, no matter the situation or the resulting consequence. I am also sure that my sister and her husband kept excellent records of those funds, just in case. But think of that for a minute: When it's your mother you're talking about, should you really ever need a "just in case"?

The end result of all of this was twofold. My sister returned the funds that our mother gave her in the first place, and then she ensured that my parents had no contact with her or her boys. Sounds fair and just, right? This had been a long time coming! Unfortunately, I also would not talk to my sister for the next ten years of my life. That sucked. Because of my mom, I lost contact with one of the only family members on my mother's side whom I cared about. I believed that my sister also just needed a break from all of it, though I would understand it differently later in life.

This whole incident, of course, had an impact on my mother's side of the family as well. She alienated herself, my father, and me from contact with most of them for good. That was not necessarily the worst thing that would happen to me, but it still hurt. As a whole, that narrow-minded group blamed me for a lot of my mother's problems and accused me of being a terrible son. *Open your eyes and look for the root of the problem*, I wanted to tell them; it wasn't me after all.

One conversation with one of my favorite aunts went something like, "You're a piss-poor excuse for a son!"

I retorted, "Well, at least I didn't throw my kids out of the house for some guy that I was shacking up with!"

Top-notch! Can you feel the heat?

What little communication my mother had with her family was spent providing them with false accusations about my father and me and how badly we treated her. What they should have done is dug a little deeper, found out the truth, and rightfully removed the thorn in everyone's side.

But wait, it gets better! My mother also tried to sue/have their license revoked/ have their children taken away from my cousins from the only aunt I really like on my mother's side. They somehow, foolishly, tried to help my mother find another house to move to. Mind you, in the twelve years my wife and I have been together, she has moved no fewer than ten times.

When my cousins tried to help my mother, she got something screwed up again and scapegoated them for her lack of knowledge and downright ignorance. Poor kids. They were just trying to get started in life, too. Just in case you are wondering, they turned out okay.

One of the worst days in my life came in December 1997, right in the midst of all of the above family conflicts. My maternal grandmother, the most wonderful woman ever, passed away on New Year's Eve. Even though I had been expecting it, her loss would be a significant to my world. I found out through my parents while I was on a ship down in the Caribbean. I decided to stay at my employ, as I had already said my good-byes and I love yous while I was at home last time between ship's contracts, but I still miss my grandma greatly to this day.

No one in her family wanted to have anything to do with my mother. She had alienated and pissed off all of them over the years, and her two recent legal moves hadn't helped her case. She had given up everything that was important to her, except money and her smoking habit. And she had already sued one child; what could she possibly do that would be worse than that? As you will soon discover, she would lose the other thing that would have meant everything to anyone else: her only son.

Chapter 13: Here Comes My Bride

A few chapters ago, I referenced my best girlfriend in the world, S1. She was a sweet, loving, and funny girl whom I had a crush on starting the first day I met her in college. She lived directly across the hall from me at SMSU. I constantly tried to court her but had zero success. No big deal—her friendship and antics kept us both smiling and laughing for the next ten years of our lives.

S1 was my confidant, a person who listened to some of the same stories of childhood abuse and neglect that I've shared in previous chapters. We had a lot of happy times together and dried a lot of each other's tears, and I thought our strong bond would last forever, but times and people change and grow in different directions, and that, unfortunately, eventually happened in our relationship.

In addition to soul sharing, we liked to play practical jokes on each other and laugh at each other's crazy antics. S1 was also the conduit through which I met my soul mate, the woman I love, cherish, respect, and adore: Becky. S1 worked with Becky at a retail shop in West County, St. Louis, and I happened to walk in at the right time one day. I was being my typical loud and obnoxious self and strolled into the store where they were working, while on my "sell" phone. (Everyone knows when I am entering a room; I'm not exactly a quiet guy.)

I can clearly recall meeting my next wife-to-be on that autumn weeknight. She was beautiful and had a smile that stopped my spinning world. I introduced myself, gave her my card, and went on about my business. That was it. I would not see or hear from her for the next year. It's a shame I wasted a year of my life without her.

Time passed, and I was becoming lonelier by the day, because I could not seem to find the right girl. Remember, I am a product of an extremely codependent couple who thrived on their hate-love relationship. I needed someone to be part of my life. I had become a bit more selective than I was in college because I knew, at least, what I did not want.

Knowing my loneliness, S1 set me up on a blind date with a random friend. We planned to all meet as a group down at a bar called the Venice Café. It was an artsy little place that I had not visited before. Upon arriving, S1 introduced me to the young lady, and we talked for a couple of minutes. Now, I am not the best-looking, most physically fit, or sexiest dude in the world, but I do groom on a regular basis and I did take a couple of minutes to get ready that night. S1's friend showed up in a pair of overalls, with messy hair and no makeup, which didn't really fly with my personal taste.

Then I saw the woman of my dreams. Becky was sitting with the group on a concrete pew. She was dressed to the hilt (highlighting her God-given curves), with her hair and makeup expertly applied. She was hot! I remembered her face from a year before, so I went over and struck up a conversation with her. I have a knack for speaking to people I know; it's the unknown ones I have problems with. But Becky was kind and patient enough to endure my flirtations. I bought her a beer (Jamaican Red Stripe), and we hung out the rest of the night. She was as sweet as could be and a great conversationalist, and she had a great sense of humor. She was also more articulate and intelligent than I at conversation, so I had to put on my deluxe-model thinking cap for her. I didn't get a college edu-ma-cation for nothin'.

During our first encounter, I saw Becky as a cute, smiling, and funny blond who could grace any room. Now I know she has an amazing charm about her that makes people grin when she speaks. She is humble and has lower-than-average self-esteem but makes up for it with an amazing personality. She is someone whom I trust wholeheartedly with my life, our kids, my business, and my friendships. She is independent, strong-willed, and caring, and the best mother you will ever find. Simply stated, she's amazing!

After that first night, we went on a couple of dates that I thought were successful. I got to kiss her, which was a lot of fun. In my opinion, we were moving along nicely. We had date nights and went out with friends. Our relationship and our social times were usually built around meals, as we both loved to eat good food. We always had fun together and made each other laugh. This girl was a true catch in every sense of the word—she was a keeper!

Then she told me not to call her again.

The reason Becky asked me not to call her is easy to admit now, but it was impossible for me to recognize back then. The fact is, I was a prick in the early days of our relationship. I was judgmental, easy to anger, and really not as nice as I could have or should have been. I cannot think of a more appropriate place to put this line: Beck, I am *so extremely sorry* for being such an asshole when I met you. You did not deserve it!

You already met Becky's mother earlier; she and my therapist are the reasons I am writing this book. Becky's father is just as wonderful. She comes from two extremely fair, loving, and compassionate parents who have, in many ways, replaced mine. (Remember the title of this book?) These are two parents whom I would have chosen if I'd had the chance. Becky was raised to be everything I wasn't, and it showed.

Unfortunately, after time, the abusive psychology that I carried with me began to transfer over to my lovely bride-to-be. When you spend continuous time with people, no matter what they are like, you begin to emulate them and become like them, to some extent. You already know my story and know I'm not an ideal person to follow, but poor Becky picked up some of my bad habits, like yelling, cursing, and alternately being on the attack and on the defensive.

I could actually see her change as we moved forward in our relationship. You may know what I'm talking about: When you first meet someone, everything is rose petals and rainbows. But as you progress over time, you begin to argue about who knows what, for God only knows what reason. The once-innocent and sweet young lady I had met had become a protégée of mine. She—and anyone else in shoes like this—did not deserve to undergo that transformation.

Becky also helped me to discover another significant negative point that came along with being in a relationship with me: I expected her to fill the void that my parents had left in my soul. Because she was such a wonderful and caring person, I thought she would be the answer to all that I have been through over the years. Not so. You cannot and should not expect your mate to replace your parents; it's just not fair. Your mate can help you identify and work through your problems, but it is not his or her job to be your parent(s).

We decided to fight through our relationship together, and believe me, it was a long uphill battle. But, as most people in this position do, you will hope that the good times will outweigh the bad and that will sooner or later wash away the bad memories. We were an abusive mess, contesting our way through the daily grind with each other and losing ourselves in angry and unwarranted arguments over trivial and pointless things. It was a complete waste of our time, but I did not know any better then; thanks to my parents' examples, I could only assume that was how it was supposed to be.

I can clearly recall one significant time when Becky's parents came over right before we got married—as great parents should—because they were worried about their daughter after a phone conversation they'd had with her. My father-in-law and I had a deep discussion about respect and the way I needed to treat a partner in a relationship. I agreed, nodded, and went on being the same asshole I had been all along. This talk did not truly hit home until about four years into our marriage.

When I asked Becky to marry me, she graciously gave me the benefit of the doubt. I was, and still am, a true romantic at heart. We were on the beach in Jamaica during a short getaway, and I had found the perfect place to propose on a pier that jutted out over the water. The waves were rolling in, the sun was setting, and there was a bucket of Red Stripe waiting for our sunset stroll. I had even hired a local guitarist,

Eddie, to play our song. It was truly a moment that she could not refuse. And yes, she said yes!

Now, my thinking was as follows: If you are having a hard time with something, then add a celebration to it, and it will only get better. Not quite true. Although we were truly in love and were destined, in some weird way, to be together forever, it was still rough. There was a lot of anger and animosity between us. We did have a solid foundation for our relationship, but it was a jagged road to get there. Oh well, we took the "red pill" and moved forward.

Of course, as time progressed, so did my abusive behavior toward Becky. I said mean and inconsiderate things designed not only to get to her and bring her down but to hurt her as well. I had learned from the best—my mother—and I was good at it. I picked out and focused on whatever hardships Becky might be having and exploited them for my benefit. What a fucking prick! Eventually, Becky became just as good at fighting as I was. There was no end to the topics we would battle over; they just came up again and again. We set each another off, said mean things, said more mean things, felt bad, and then apologized.

If you learn one thing from this book, please remember that an apology can put a Band-Aid on a cut, but it *will not* heal a broken heart and soul. The words and actions that you use against another person can be forgiven but *never* forgotten. Don't ever dismiss this from your mind. Say only what you mean and have to say, or don't say it at all. As I quoted my friend Cali's grandmother earlier in the book, "Keep your words soft and sweet, because someday you might have to eat them." This is especially true when dealing with your loved ones.

We were a year into our marital relationship when Becky became pregnant. My daughter was born on the day one of our former illustrious leaders in the White House decided to start a war that his daddy couldn't win. She was absolutely a beautiful baby— cute, snuggly, and quiet. My, how things change (at least the "quiet" part).

Noelle is an amazing child with a heart of pure gold. This kid will do whatever it takes to make sure that the other party is pleased before her needs are met. She's a little bit of a snot now, but she's ten—what do you expect? Still, you won't find a more considerate or loving soul. She is beautiful in every way, and I love her to pieces.

This amazing bundle of joy brought Becky and me to a whole new level in our relationship, but the peace we found did not last for long, because I still had not owned up to the fact that I was abusive, like my parents, and had done nothing to fix it. I was still blaming Becky for everything and not taking any responsibility for the shit that I did wrong. There was no escaping this circle that had us tied down.

But the older and wiser I became, the more I learned that some things need to be left up to professionals. We tried alone to fix things, but they only became worse. So, after one of our heated battles, Becky decided it was time to pack up and get out of the house with the baby, and she left. Good for her. I deserved it. By doing the right thing, she saved our marriage and our lives and began to put an end to the cycle of abuse that had been handed down from generation to generation in my family. It was high time for a change.

If you are stuck in an abusive relationship that is beyond repair, then maybe it is time for a break for you as well. If you leave, either way, be ready for repercussions. Your mate probably won't like it, as I didn't. *But*, do what you have to do to protect you and yours. Simply said, if you have to get out to protect yourself and your children, then do what you have to do. Safety first.

Chapter 14: Starting to Stop

It was a *very* long month when Becky and the baby went to Becky's parents' home to stay and take a much-needed break from me, for her safety and the safety of our child. Each of the violent arguments we had been having for months had escalated our emotions and increased her fear of me, even physically. I never did raise a hand to her but rather took out my anger on glass photo frames, walls, doors, chairs, etc. What a redneck! I was a ticking time bomb, ready to explode at the slightest provocation.

At first, I felt angry, hurt, vengeful, and sad. I thought *I* was teaching Becky a lesson, because our separation was "completely her fault." I did not know what to do with myself except to build a large deck onto the back of our house and think about all she had done to cause this. I mean, this most certainly would not have happened if she had been better at being a wife.

But soon after that, the words from the '80s Cinderella song began to ring true: "Don't know what you got till it's gone," and I started my path toward understanding that *I* was responsible for adding so much fuel to our blazing fire. I began to beg and plead for Becky to come back. I tried over and over to persuade her, but the time was just not right—for either of us, it turns out.

In one desperate attempt to recourt my wife and get her back into our house. I met her for lunch, and all I could do was cry and petition her to come back . . . but she took the advice of her (and my) friends and stayed away. I then went through a determined and frantic series of attempts to show her how I was hurting. We drove by our old house for memories, drove by the psych ward that I spoke of in earlier chapters, and even went by all of our favorite St. Louis hot spots—all in a vain attempt to rekindle what I had screwed up. But Becky was strong and stuck with the program. Good for her!

In the meantime, I was busy blaming her, feeling sorry for myself, and trying to put the pieces of my broken heart and spirit back together. It became evident to me that I needed to change my approach and focus to win her heart back. I had broken it, and that was not a good thing.

We began seeking out counselors at our church, and a few friends suggested other ones, and finally we met Dr. Tina Reising. She was the one who not only talked but listened. Rather than taking sides, she presented solutions to us and allowed us to make a decision. It was in her office and during this separation that I learned that I was an abusive man toward both Becky and our daughter and that I needed to change. *I* was the one causing the pain; my wife was just reacting to it. Just like my parents before me, it was all me!

Now, this is not to say that my wife got off the hook completely. Trust me, Becky is a shit-stirrer as well. She likes to give me problems and instigate things at random. Her worst quality is that once an uncomfortable situation is complete, she will drag it out and punish me for the fact that it happened for hours, maybe even days. But she's only human, too. No one is perfect.

It was also in Dr. Tina's office that we found out that I have bipolar disorder, a neurological dysfunction that induces extreme states of mania and depression, all caused by the body's chemical imbalance. I, like my parents (especially my mother), was screwed up. Great—now I'd never get to be president or fly a plane. You can't be a psycho and rule the free world . . . right?

It was also during this time that Becky became stronger as a woman and wife and decided she would not tolerate any more of my shit. The abuse cycle was to end here, or we would not continue as husband and wife. I decided—and I had to be the one to make this decision—that she and Noelle were worth keeping and that I would do whatever it took to make the necessary changes to hold on to them. It was time for me to move forward and finally grow. No more excuses! The grocery list Becky gave me to check off before she would come back included counseling and therapy, medication for my disorder, and stopping the cycle that my parents had instilled in me for thirty-plus years.

I have spoken a great deal about Becky in this chapter but have not forgotten about my amazing daughter Noelle. As I have said before, you will not find a sweeter or more caring, fun, and creative girl than this young woman. She would do anything for anyone and suffer the consequences later. Amazing! But my problems and the problems that Becky and I had did have a serious impact on my little girl.

Noelle was sad at times, and once I stepped back and realized that it was I who helped to create this undesired emotion, I felt not only guilty but also responsible for my actions, and rightly so. This child should have had a carefree upbringing in a fun and relaxed atmosphere; instead she grew up in a thick forest of emotional abuse surrounding her mommy. I can say with confidence that I never did directly aim any abuse at my daughter, but, sadly, she was there to witness and receive the runoff from me to Mom. I am sorry, little girl. I love you so much!

My wife and daughters would experience what I had gone through with the same negative drive and lack of focus that my parents did with me. Nothing had changed; everything was the same. The only difference is that I made the decision to stop this vicious cycle and make it better for them, and for myself. It was then that life became better for everyone, and I learned that most of that was within my control.

Now, the changes that I have indicated did not come easily; my years of abuse were etched into my soul as just how things should be. Abuse came out just as readily as the words "I love you." I had learned the gift of being able to talk out of both sides of my mouth at the same time. It was a long and winding road (thanks, Paul!), but the changes I made did slowly come to fruition.

A "real man" will do whatever is necessary to protect, provide for, and give love to his family. In my case, I understand now that a "real man" would not pass on the abuse to his family. A "real man" would end the cycle once and for all. It doesn't matter how big your mullet is, how much camouflage you wear, how big your truck tires are, how big your muscles are, or whatever other bullshit excuse you can come up with—if you want to be a "real man," then fulfill the promises that you made on your wedding day (if you are married) and fix what you can *now*! Don't wait another minute and put it off till next time. Change starts now!

There is an outdated saying in the psychology field that it takes twenty-one days to change a habit. I am here to tell you from firsthand experience that, while I do believe many things I read in books, twenty-one days is far from realistic. After thirty years of tormented abuse, both physical and especially emotional, I promise you that it is still an ongoing process.

On your journey, if you decide to take it, you will find that it is much easier to fall back into your old ways, old habits, and the old you than it is to face the challenges before you. Regrettably, it is safe to say that you will have relapses, but you must make the decision to put a stop to this struggle and become someone new. Do this for yourself first and your life partner (if you have one) second. This must be for you! Go ahead and be a little selfish—you deserve it!

When Becky did finally return to what I had vowed to transform from a house into a home, believe you me, I welcomed her. We had a lot of dirty laundry to air—both clothes and emotions—but we agreed together to give it another shot. Things would finally take a turn for the best. I was going to start fresh and make things happen, and my determination was set in stone! We knew this attitude would add a whole new, bright chapter to the book of our family.

My parents, however, did not agree with what was about to happen. You have to remember that my mother and father were comfortable with who and what they were, and are, and were not about to make any changes for me, or themselves. They would resist what was to come and denounce the idea as bad. Their incredulity marked the end of their regime and the start of a new democracy . . . almost.

I say "almost" because my parents still had a few tricks of blame up their sleeve to sling around. They blamed Becky and her parents for leading me to the "dark" side of change and still claimed their own thoughts, belief systems, and way of life were true and just. They even told me that Becky could not "destroy the close family bond that we have." I heard more about how I was going to hell and how I was so wrong for what I was doing—becoming a better person and all.

On my journey, I fell short of promises and guarantees many times. It was the hardest thing I had ever done. There were two key aspects of the process I had to look at: I *had* to do it, and *I* had to do it. In the first example, I truly didn't have a choice in the matter; I *had* to either change or lose the greatest gifts my God ever gave me. The second statement holds just as much weight: it was *I* who had to make things happen. It was not Becky's responsibility to pick up the pieces, but she made the choice to do so and therefore made it somewhat easier on me. I love and appreciate her so much for making that sacrifice. Thank you, my love.

Bullshit!

It was time! It was time for the changes that had needed to take place for so many years to happen.

It was time for the abusive cycle that I had learned and mastered to be broken. It was time for me to grow up, accept responsibility for my actions, and be a "real man." It was finally time for me to have what I had wanted all along: a real home and family!

Chapter 15: I Made It. So Can You!

"Do your best to be someone others would like to be."

—Scotty O'Brien, two minutes ago, upstairs recliner

The old saying "He who dies with the most toys, wins" isn't true after all. I believe the journey—the life experiences—that it takes to get all the toys is far more important. This is what makes the difference! Your job on Earth is to take care of yourself first and those around you second. I know that may be a little contrary to what your belief system may tell you, but if you are reading this book, it is for a reason. Take care of yourself first, and then solve the problems for the rest of the world. You deserve time to heal and rebuild from the abuse that you encountered. Take care of you!

Remember when I said we are not here to compete, but to share stories. The same holds true now at the end of the book. Your stories may have been much more painful and traumatic than mine were, but I just wanted to share with you what I went through. Please take it all in and know that it hurt, but I have now overcome my past and am enjoying life can truly offer.

I also understand that you may be in a particular funk right now, or in the middle of trying to make your life a bit better, but might be having difficulty finding the way to fulfill that goal. No problem! When you have everything under control and in perspective, it will all make much more sense.

I have come full circle in my lifetime of physical, verbal, and emotional abuse. I have been on both sides of the river: that of the abused and that of the abuser. It has taken me forty long years to figure out what is right and what is not, and it has been a strenuous journey. But in the end, I made it! I have come to find out that I was not to blame for all of my parents' problems, wrongdoings, and faults. Their problems were *their* issues and not *my* fault.

It also took me a long time to figure out that I cannot be held responsible for what they went through when they grew up, what they put me through when I was growing up, or what they still do to this day. They were consenting adults, while I was just a child who really had no say and simply had to suffer the consequences.

You must make changes to your perspective and actions, similar to the way I did, in order to improve your quality of life. If you want things to get better, then you must first decide that you cannot be held responsible for someone else's actions toward you during your formative and later years, no matter how much guilt and weight that person put on your shoulders. This is not only your cross to bear; you don't have to go it alone.

Parents just like mine will say that their abusive behavior is just and right and that they can't help it. Wrong! Take the feelings that you are using to console them and use that energy for yourself. It is a harder task than you think, but well worth the effort.

The human ability to adapt to the most egregious of circumstances and to then consider those circumstances the "norm" is truly amazing. Fortunately, we are able to learn from the mistakes of those around us, as well as our own, and to change our behavior for both our own betterment and that of future generations. Changing happens spontaneously for some and over a long period of time for others. At one point or another, you will finally get it—something will click, and then you will know it is time to change. Your job is to listen for that clicking sound.

If your cycle of abuse continues into the years when you *can* make decisions to finally get out of the abusive situation, then it may become your responsibility to do so. There is only so much that children can do when they are living under their parents' roof, but once you are able to start making wise decisions for yourself, do the right thing. I promise it will be better for you and those around you.

It is also not your responsibility or problem to try to improve the life of your parents (or whoever damaged you). You will have a big enough job taking care of your own stuff, much less theirs as well. Give your abusers the number of a good counselor and hope for the best. Your job right now is *you*! They did what they could do by making it harder for you; now overcome that challenge and become a better person for you and yours.

Please note that there is a very good chance that the responsible party will reject, rather than embrace, the newfound you. They will not like the changes that you are trying to make, nor will welcome your efforts, because they go against the grain of how your abusers treated and raised you. As in my case, they may even turn on you. It is up to you to decide how much, or how little, change you are ready to make. You will soon find out the true colors of your abusers' spirits when all of this takes place. It will not be easy, but anything worth getting and keeping never is.

The next step is to find someone whom you can trust with your deepest feelings and secrets. *Do not* go to a friend and think that this will solve the issues. It is not fair to your friend, or to you, to expect those answers. In the end, you may be sharing more than that person needs to know or can handle . . . and you may lose that friend in the end.

I would recommend a professional who works with victims of abuse, because that person will just listen and will not be biased and judging about what you are going to share with them. Take the time to find someone you are comfortable with. If you do not like the first person you meet, keep looking; you will find the right one eventually. Sometimes the setting for therapy may even be a group situation. You will know when you have found your book of answers.

Also, do not be afraid of or embarrassed about searching for and needing help on this road away from abuse. You needed someone to help cause this problem, so why shouldn't you have someone there to help fix it? Getting help does not mean that you are weak. Quite the opposite! It means that you are going to be something different than what you came from, and that is good! After the healing process begins, no matter how long it may take, you can begin to make changes to your life for a new and better you.

Think of it as painting an old house. You have to strip the old paint away to get to the original wood, which is typically beautiful and ready to go. Sometimes this wood may be damaged and have some splinters and knots in it. No problem—just replace the board with another one. There is no telling how long this will take (I guess it depends on how big the house is), but after you remove all of the old paint, you can start fresh and new. Start with a color that you like and that you will enjoy and be proud of. Hey, man, this is your frickin' house anyway. Please know that shedding and releasing the pain that has been dealt to you may not always be a delight, so get ready for some tears and some relief at the same time. Just please remember this was *not* your fault.

There will be times when you will feel like you are getting nowhere, or even going backward. Try harder and keep your focus. Seek professional help. Don't give up. This will be one of the most important things, if not *the* most important thing, that you do in your life. Your choice is simple: either heal or continue living with all of this wonderful fucking baggage that your abusers gave you, and that you don't deserve.

You will become bare and vulnerable during this process, so keep your guard up. In other words, your abusers taught you how to abuse and will enjoy that you are heading down the same path as they were—unless they hear a *click*, too. They do not want to see you stray from them or their ways. So protect yourself and remain strong throughout this growing and healing journey.

My parents knocked me down again and again as I evolved, but with the help of Becky, my counselor, and a few choice others, I made it. Once I recognized that I had become my parents and that it was time for a change, that was the gas that fueled my fire.

Some of you may have no idea that you are being abused, because everything seems the way it should be in your house. You will have more of a struggle than others because of this perception. You must first admit it, own it, and embrace it; only then you can heal. So make sure that you are ready before you start this journey.

Finally, once you do start, *do not stop*! The healing process can take a mighty long time to work through, and sometimes it is ongoing. I know mine is. I screw up again and again and rebound back into my own ways. Then I stop and think to myself that this is not who I want to be for either my family or for me. I want to be different and provide them with the unconditional and incredible love that I know I am capable of providing. Yes, your abuse hurt you deeply, but life is not over yet. Grasp that pain and change it into something positive and new.

One more reminder that this process will take time, and lots of it. Forty years of abuse and anger and hate all took their toll on me. Now that I have separated myself from this negativity and know what is good and what is not, it is not so hard. Just stick with it, and never quit. You will be amazed at and proud of what you can become!

Chapter 16: From the N-Word to the P-Word—
Where Are We Now?

When I bought my first house, Becky came over and cleaned, organized, and helped put everything away. (Wonder what happened to that woman!) I had asked my parents to come over and give a hand as well, so we did it on an off weekend. Becky had just finished the kitchen and I was working on the garage when they showed up. My dad helped me work on shelving for storage in the garage, and my mother told us what we were doing wrong, as usual.

Becky had just finished wiping out the cabinets and told my mother this. My mother's reply was, "Good. I thought I was going to have to hire a [insert off-color racist remark here] to do that work." My wife was floored. This was the first ten minutes of meeting my parents. Poor Becky!

So, where are we now, you may ask? Becky, my two daughters, and I are doing wonderfully. We have two not-so-bright dogs and still live in Missouri most of the time. I travel quite a bit for work and still love my job. The best part of it all is the vacations that we get to spend together, away from everything. I love bonding with and getting to know my girls more and more each day and teaching them things that I have been taught . . . differently.

You will be pleased to know that things are way different from what I grew up with. I still have ups and downs because of my bipolar disorder, but I am medicated to help smooth things out. I still see Dr. Tina on a very regular basis, but now we spend time reading this book and talking about it and growing from that experience. I am well into my healing process, but it is far from over. I am not sure if it ever will be, but I am excited to be at a point where I might be able to help someone else—hence this book.

My mother is constantly in and out of hospitals, using the system to get what she wants and taking advantage of whoever she can to move things along in her direction. I bought her a house with money that she "gifted" me, helped her with the loan, etc; she then decided to not pay me back, or her bills, as promised, so I was stuck with that.

I also had to take out a restraining order against my mother when she threatened my life, and my father's, a couple of years or so ago. That was right after she got in Becky's face, physically threatening her as well. She did everything short of push Becky while my wife was holding our then year-old.

Before that, I tried and tried to give my mother chances at changing and becoming a better person, but that just wasn't happening. Against everyone's advice, I would forgive and understand and try to move forward again and again. It never worked. She would always rebound right back into her abusive behavior.

I think the worst thing that my mother and father share is their lack of a relationship with my daughters. They seem to have no interest in spending time with my girls, even when they were younger. I thought grandparents were supposed to bite at every chance they could to see their grandkids! Instead, all we've gotten are broken promises and selfish accusations that I am not going to put my daughters through anymore. Becky and I have initiated some of the distance from my parents, but this has been a conscious decision for the safety and well-being of our girls. Our job is to protect them and provide for them as best we possibly can.

I do sometimes wonder if my parents miss me, if they are sorry, or if they even care. Knowing my mother, I am sure it will always be my fault for everything that ever happened. If she blamed me when I was a young boy for starting her fights and disagreements with my dad, why not continue the cycle now?

My father and I talk regularly and stay in touch. Please remember, he is not mean-spirited like his better half. But he still goes back again and again for more and more of the punishment of being with her. Very lonely, I guess. I am the same way—I need constant companionship—but I have chosen a healthier alternative to fulfill my needs.

How about another story to cap things off? My mother was invited to Becky's bridal shower around eleven years ago and sat next to one of Becky's best friends, who wasn't expecting my mother to tell her a story about my ex-girlfriend's stinky vagina and what a slut she was. Great timing, as usual, Mother.

It's about time to wrap this deal up. Thank you for allowing me to share some of the stories of my life with you. My original goal was to write this book and get it out on paper and out of my system, but my real hope in writing it is to also help others who are going or have gone through what I have. Fortunately or unfortunately, we have shared something similar, so I hope my stories helped you, if only a little bit.

Remember, keep on trying and never give up. You will make it and become who you truly want to become. You will heal from the hurt. Good luck and God bless!

Acknowledgements

There are a great number of people that I need to thank for making this project possible, so I will list them in no particular order. First off, my parents. I mean, without them I would not have had all of this bullshit to write about, and I guess I would have had a semi-normal life like the rest of the kids that I watched grow up. Who knows? Maybe I am the normal one and they were all of the screwed-up ones. Anyway, thank you Mom and Dad.

I will note again that my mother and I still to this day do not talk and will probably never talk again. It took me a long time to figure out that there are just some people that will never change and she is the one in my life. I will just keep her in my prayers and hope the best for the rest of her life that she has created.

My father and I do spend time together on a regular basis and I am actually hoping that we can become closer once again. I took a needed break from both of the parents to write this book and to evaluate my pain and figure out where I truly was in life. But no matter what I have written, remember, my father at least consistently tried. Out of the two parents, he did what he could with what he had to make it work for me. Thank you for that, Dad.

Next in line would be my best friend and life support system, Becky. My wife has endured the brunt of all of this crap and has tolerated and stuck with me through thick and thin. She deserves a medal. You cannot imagine the verbal and emotional fights that we have been through to get where we are today. Thank you for sticking with me for the blessed outcome. Thank you for being my everything, for pushing me to complete this project, for enduring all of the tears that went along with it and for listening to it over and over. You are simply amazing.

Thank you to my girls, Noelle and Layla for putting up with me for the start of your lives up until now. Daddy loves you both so much and would do anything for you. The first gift that I will give you is the gift of not putting you through what I had to go through when I was a kid. The cycle has stopped and the spell has been broken. No one deserves it.

Noelle, a special thanks to you for always being supportive when I was learning to stop the cycle. I am so sorry that sometimes everything may not have been as peaceful for you as it should have been, but I was learning. I love you.

Thank you God for answering prayers and never letting me down. Ever!

Jonathan, Cali, The Surfing Senator! Brother, thank you for spending your precious time from your family on this project and helping me with the first round of... edits! Thank you for reading my story and always being there for me, no matter what. And most of all, thank you for your years of dedication. I will look forward to growing old with you, my proven friend.

On the note of editing, a very special thank you to Brooke and Annie for taking the time out of your lives to make this project understandable to the rest of the world. Your support made me smile big time!

Tim, thank you for always being there for me and *never* letting me down.

Thank you to all of my other friends and family that have helped nudge me down the right path. You are all loved.

Karyl... not only my mother-in-law, but an amazing friend. Thank you for pushing me to become better and actually reaching for what I am capable of. I could not have done it without you. I am also sure that you will continue to be my guiding light through the rest of my career as husband and father. Thank you so much, I love you!

Dr. Tina Reising. Wow! We made it! Without the help of Dr. Reising and her strong, secure and reassuring words, I would still be an abusive asshole. Thank you for making sure that I did not give up, for always being there for me and for standing with my family as an angel on our side.

Finally, I will dedicate this book to you, the reader. If you went through even a portion of what I did then you deserve this. May your life get better, your words become sweeter and your abuse be overcome.

Notes